The Stacions of Rome,

Pilgrims Sea-Voyage,

and

Clene Maydenhod.

The Stacions of Rome,

(In Verse from the Vernon MS., ab. 1370 A.D., and in Prose from the Porkington MS. No. 10, ab. 1460-70 A.D.,)

and the

Pilgrims Sea-Voyage:

(From the Trin. Coll., Cambridge, MS. R, 3, 19, t. Hen. VI.)

with

Clene Maydenhod.

(From the Vernon MS., ab. 1370 A.D., in the Bodleian Library, Oxford.)

A SUPPLEMENT TO "POLITICAL, RELIGIOUS, AND LOVE POEMS,"
AND "HALI MEIDENHAD,"
(Early English Text Society, 1866.)

EDITED BY

FREDERICK J. FURNIVALL, M.A.,
TRIN. HALL, CAMBRIDGE.

LONDON:
PUBLISHED FOR THE EARLY ENGLISH TEXT SOCIETY,
BY N. TRÜBNER & CO., 60, PATERNOSTER ROW.

MDCCCLXVII.

Great Clarendon Street, Oxford OX2 6DP
United Kingdom

Oxford University Press is a department of the University of Oxford.
It furthers the University's objective of excellence in research, scholarship,
and education by publishing worldwide. Oxford is a registered trade mark of
Oxford University Press in the UK and in certain other countries

© The Early English Text Society 1867

The moral rights of the authors have been asserted

Database right Oxford University Press (maker)

First Edition published in 1867

All rights reserved. No part of this publication may be reproduced,
stored in a retrieval system, or transmitted, in any form or by any means,
without the prior permission in writing of Oxford University Press,
or as expressly permitted by law, or under terms agreed with the appropriate
reprographics rights organization. Enquiries concerning reproduction
outside the scope of the above should be sent to the Rights Department,
Oxford University Press, at the address above

You must not circulate this book in any other form
and you must impose this same condition on any acquirer

Published in the United States of America by Oxford University Press
198 Madison Avenue, New York, NY 10016, United States of America

British Library Cataloguing in Publication Data
Data available

Library of Congress Cataloging in Publication Data
Data available

Original Series, 25

ISBN 978-0-85-991812-1

PREFACE.

THE Catalogue that Mr Halliwell printed of the contents of the Vernon MS. was, unluckily, one of his own making, and not a copy of that prefixed to the magnificent Southern-dialect volume by the Scribe who wrote it, and which will, I hope, be printed in the next Text that the Society issues from this MS. One result of the non-publication of it before, was, that when searching for other copies of the *Stacyons of Rome*, for the volume of "Political, Religious, and Love Poems," edited by me in the early part of this year for the Society, I saw nothing like the *Stacyons* in the printed Catalogue, and felt sure that the Poem was not in the Vernon MS., notwithstanding Mr Halliwell's warning that his notices "must be accepted as very imperfect." But as there were two entries in that gentleman's Catalogue of "117, *Short Religious Poems*, f. 298, r° β. ; 128, *Short Religious Poems*, fol. 319, r° a," and I had long contemplated continuing the small instalment of these pieces edited by me for the Philological Society (Trans. Pt. II., 1858), I commissioned our Oxford copier to transcribe from the MS. the first and last lines, and burdens if any, of all these Short Poems. The execution of the order was delayed for some months, but when it was completed, and I was turning over the leaves of the copy, what should appear on three of the foolscap sheets, for fol. 314, r° γ, to fol. 315 r° γ, of the MS., but the first and last lines of the different paragraphs of the *Stations*,— thus explaining Mr Halliwell's entry, "Short Religious Poems." A longish piece, evidently A Dialogue between the Virgin and the

vi PREFACE.

Cross of Christ, followed, treated in the same way. What was to be done? Nothing but groan, say "mistakes are natural to man" (I know they are to me), and print the earlier text. Here accordingly it is, and printed with all its metrical points, and guard-stops on each side of figures and single letters, as in the MS., for an experiment how Members like these points and stops reproduced.

This early Vernon version has not several passages which later transcribers have introduced into the Cotton and Lambeth MSS. It shows that the Lambeth continuation of the Cotton MS. was not a late addition, but that the Cotton had lost its tail. It shows the Lambeth text to be more like it than the Cotton, in the passages which all three contain; and though it does not clear up any of the puzzles of the later copies, it is interesting, as well for its earlier language as for the new Churches it mentions. These are eleven in number,

St Anthony's, l. 473
St Martin's in the Mount, l. 563
St Marcelle's, l. 609
St Grisogon's, l. 680
St Tyre and St John's, l. 681
St Angelo's, l. 693

St Adrian's, l. 701
St Clement's, l. 704
St Stephen's, l. 705
The Virgin's Chapel, where Thomas à Becket kept school, l. 717
St Urban's, l. 720

and on them Mr William M. Rossetti has, as on those of the former volume, kindly added notes, which follow this Preface. Thus far I had written when I learnt from Sir F. Madden's Appendix to his Preface to his *Syr Gawayne* that (the late) Mr Ormsby Gore's Porkington MS. No. 10, contained a copy of the *Stations* in prose, beginning "In Rome bethe ii⁣ᶜ paresche churchs." I at once applied for leave to see the MS., and the present Mr Ormsby Gore forthwith obtained it for me from his mother. Its *Stacyons* proved to be a short and incomplete abstract of our long Poem, in 7½ pages of a very small MS., wisely wound up with an *Et C.*, and I have therefore printed it here for completeness and contrast sake.

The allusion to the sea-voyage to the Holy Land in the *Stations*,

3if men wuste . grete and smale
þe pardoun þat is . at grete Rome.

þei wolde tellen . In heore dome.
Hit were no neod . to mon in cristiante
To passe in to þe holy lond . ouer þe séé.
To Jerusalem . ne to kateryne.

has induced me to add to this Text the most amusing Poem on "The Pilgrims' Sea-Voyage and Sea-Sickness," from MS. Trin. Coll., Camb., R. 3, 19, first printed by Mr Halliwell in *Reliquiæ Antiquæ*, vol. 1, p. 2, 3, and to which the present Keeper of the Printed Books in the British Museum, Mr Thomas Watts—encyclopædic in knowledge and gracious in speech—called my attention some twenty years ago. Mr Aldis Wright has himself read the transcript with the MS., and I do not think that any readers will regret its reproduction here.

The cause of *Clene Maydenhod* appearing in this Text is Mr Cockayne's edition of that most vivid sketch of an English girl's temptations to forsake marriage and maternity in 1220 A.D., *Hali Meidenhad*. It is long since I have been so interested in any treatise; and seeing that *Clene Maydenhod* was in the Vernon, I could not resist the temptation of printing it, for illustration and contrast sake. The texts are paged separately, so that they may be bound, if wished, with those that they refer to ; and for the same reason the Index to the names of Men and Churches in *Stations* refers to the Cotton and Lambeth versions printed in " Political, Religious, and Love Poems," 1866. Mr George Parker, of Rose Hill, Oxford, has read both the Vernon texts with the MS., and my thanks are due to him for his care.

3, St George's Square, N.W.,
Dec., 1866.

P.S.—The reviewer in *The Saturday Review* of Dec. 22, 1866, does not understand in what sense we publish our Texts. We print them mainly for our Members ; but, remembering the times when we wanted single volumes of the books of the Camden and Percy Societies, the Abbotsford, Bannatyne and other Clubs, and could not get them, we resolved, when starting the Society, to sell each of our texts separately to any person wanting it, at the publisher's profit on its cost: this—though it would be a great nuisance to us by spoiling our sets—to benefit some poor students who might need help. We sell, perhaps, an average of five copies of each Text separately, against 400 odd issued to Members. This is why I conceive myself entitled to write Prefaces as to a circle of my friends; for such I look on Subscribers as being. Did I consider a Saturday Reviewer and the public as part of my audience, I should certainly write in a different tone to them. To the Saturday man I should say, that the libertinism* of his comments was often unworthy of a Free man;

* This called forth the following remarks—reprinted with the heading, "*The Saturday's* Insolence and *The Saturday's* Ignorance"—from one of our literary journals now discontinued: "Last Saturday's *Punch* contains the following paragraph (p. 35, col. 2, No. 349):—'Some fiddler advertises himself in the *Musical World* as 'Paganini Redividus.' One would not notice his blunder but for his cheek.' That is our own feeling about a ludicrous blunder occurring in a review of Dr Kingsley's 'Thynne on Chaucer,' in the *Saturday Review* of the week before, written in that tone of ungentlemanlike assumption and petulant insolence for which one writer, at least, in that journal has long been notorious, and which, at a certain period of its existence, drove men like Professor Pearson and Mr Bowen from its columns. Dr Kingsley—evidently not a careful corrector of the press—passed over his printer's error of printing the Anglo-Saxon thorn, or sharp *th*, þ, as *r*, p. For this he was jeered at by his reviewer in the regular vulgar-little-boy fashion; and then, by way of displaying his own learning, the little boy went on to explain the difference between *th* and *r*. But as strutting daws unwittingly drop the peacock's feathers out of their tails, so this unlucky boy either did not know, or did not notice, that he or his printer had put an Anglo-Saxon *w* (p) for the *th* (þ); so that there, while he (the clever reviewer) was pointing at Dr Kingsley for his ignorance or carelessness, he was all the time displaying his own, and deliberately forcing every one's attention to the display. Scholars at the Museum, Bodleian, Cambridge, Lambeth, and elsewhere, have enjoyed the self-inflicted punishment that the reviewer's nasty-tempered notice of a book by a courteous, well-read, and widely-esteemed gentleman and man of letters has met with. We make it public on *Punch's* principle—'One would not notice his blunder but for his cheek;'—but we trust we shall have no more such exhibitions in the *Saturday's* pages; and for the benefit of the reviewer we reprint for him the judgment he passed on his better,—commending to him the study of his 'Anglo-Saxon Grammar,' the 'Printer's Guide,' and '*The Book of Courtesy*.'—Of course, we shall be told that all these things are trifles [one 'thing' was the putting a comma for a full stop], most likely misprints. We answer that accuracy and inaccuracy are not trifles, and that a [writer] of a philological [review], who is either so ignorant that he cannot read his text, or so careless that he lets pass misprints which turn that text into nonsense, displays exactly the same *crassa ignorantia* as an architect who can do everything except build a house, or a surgeon who can do everything except cut off a leg."—*The Reader*, Feb. 3, 1866. What wonder that this man calls my masterly

that wandering through Summer Meads he should be greeted in eye and ear by sights and sounds that should bring him into sweet accord with them, and prevent his always printing every "nasty-tempered" thing he can lay tongue on; that instead of leaving a set of men— of whom the chief workers are all poorer than himself—to do a work of much help to him, without his help, but with his sneers, it would be more like a generous gentleman to send his subscription to the Society, and print a text for it with his *Saturday* pay. I should ask of the chief Cook who presides over the making of the weekly pudding that tickles so many palates and disturbs so many inwards, that he should pick out the bits of grit in the dab of pabulum contributed to his seventh-day compound by the reviewer I have been addressing. To the public on the other hand I should say, what a very stupid public it is for not supporting more vigorously the best and most liberal Early English printing Society that has ever existed: that there are several thousand well-to-do men in this country who can easily spare a guinea a year each to make their forefathers' speech and thoughts better known to this and future generations; and they ought so to spare it. To the Historian and Antiquary the Society's work yields rich fruit; to the Tory who glories in the past, it appeals with strongest claim; to the Liberal who pleads, as cause for modern justice, the ancient tale of poor men's wrongs that starts before the Conquest, the Society makes heard the voice he listens for. Every man of culture is bound to support us; and yet hardly any do. The Sanskrit Text Society starts—most rightly—with a first year's subscription of over £1200. The Early English Text Society with a miserable £152. In its third year its income is not much over £600; and when it asks for money to print nineteen Texts in one year, it hardly gets money for eleven. The apathy of English lettered men on this subject is a disgrace to them; and a journal like *The Saturday*, which has a chance of rousing them from it, would be much better employed in

strokes of irony (N.B.), nonsense, and my brilliant satire (N.M.), bad jokes? When you hear a little boy on Hampstead Heath call to a known cross-country rider, "Why don't you get inside?", need you ask whether the ingenuous youth is a judge of a seat, or is—a little boy?

doing so than in picking out little blemishes in the Society's Texts, and holding them up to show off a reviewer's fancied cleverness, which, as has been shown in some instances, and can be shown in others, has often turned out to be ludicrous ignorance. If we (as we do) point out some of our own shortcomings, we are thankful enough to have others shown us in the right spirit and the right way. The wrong in both,* I for one will protest against as best I can.

F. J. F.

* The later review of Mr Perry's edition of Hampole's *Short Prose Treatises* is written in the right and gentleman-like spirit.

NOTES ON THE STACIONS OF ROME,

By W. M. ROSSETTI.

THE notes which I wrote to the previous publication of the Early English Text Society, the "Stacyons of Rome" printed from the Cotton and Lambeth MSS., apply in great part to the present earlier version of the same poem from the Vernon MS. There are, however, considerable differences of detail between the MSS., of most of which I must leave the reader to take count for himself; and some churches, not named at all in the previously published version, are mentioned in the one now printed. On these churches, and on another point or two here and there, I proceed to offer a few notes upon the same plan as in the former instance.

Line 40. I must take this opportunity to rectify a slip of the pen in my notes upon the Cotton MS. copy, at the corresponding line, No. 56. The altar mentioned in that line is to "Seynt Symon," or, in the Lambeth and the present Vernon MSS., to " Seint Symon & Jude ; " I made the slip of saying that the Cotton MS. specified an altar " to St Jude."

Lines 55-6. The statement here made is that St Peter's Basilica was consecrated "Of Seint Martin þat eiʒteþe day." In the Cotton MS., lines 121-2, this same statement is made concerning the Basilica of San Paolo fuori le Mura; and St Peter's is stated on the contrary to have been consecrated " On Seynt Petur & Powle day." It appears that the Vernon MS. is correct, and that the two statements made in the Cotton MS. ought to be inverted.

Line 118. *Scala Celi.* Compare this from " God speed the Plough,"
> Then commeth prestis that goth to rome.
> For to haue siluer to singe at Scala celi.
> *Lansdowne MS.*, 762, *fol.* 6.

Line 126. " In tyme of *Tibian* þe Emperour." This potentate, unrecorded by historians, in whose reign 10,000 martyrs suffered in Rome, may perhaps be conjectured to be nominally compounded out of Tiberius, Trajan, and Julian—

a very Cerberus of tyranny, persecution, and apostasy. The Cotton MS. limit
itself to the first of these three, " Tyberye "—whose reign was assuredly fre
from any such wholesale persecution.

Line 160. The " holy bones" here named are to be understood as the
bones of Sts Peter and Paul. As I pointed out in my former notes, neither
the Cotton MS. in saying that these bones lay undiscovered 500 years, nor
yet the Vernon MS. in assigning 100 years as the period, can be trusted : the
true time being probably more like 19 months.

Lines 183-4 speak of 44 martyr popes who " liueden " in a chapel in the
catacombs ; in the Cotton MS. it is 46 martyr popes who "lyene" there. I
presume that "lyene" is the correct word—if indeed any item of so preposterous an assertion can be termed correct.

Lines 333-4 speak of

"þe cloþ þat crist was wounden Inne
Whon he was child for monnes sinne ; "

which seems to mean the swaddling-clothes of the Nativity. These lines correspond to 426-7 in the Cotton MS.,

" And þe cloþis þat criste was wonden In
When he shulde dye for mannis syn" ;

this latter statement appears to be the more correct, the actual object in question being the face-cloth.

Lines 357-8. According to the position of these lines in the context, the
heads of Sts Peter and Paul were under the high altar in the Chapel Sancta
Sanctorum in the old Lateran Palace of the Popes. It may be inferred that
the lines have slipped a little out of their proper place ; and that the high
altar really spoken of is that of the Basilica of St John Lateran, which would
make the statement about the heads correct. These heads were discovered
in or about 1365, in the reign of Pope Urban V., which commenced in 1362.
The date of the Vernon MS. is about 1370, when the discovery must still have
been an interesting novelty to actual or intending pilgrims to Rome : and, in
accordance with this date, we find that the lines of the Cotton MS., 456-9,

"There ys no man now y-bore," &c.,

which my previous notes cited for the purpose of fixing the date of that MS.
at not later than 1445, do not appear at all in the Vernon version of the poem.

Line 427. The Church here (and also in the Lambeth MS.) named " of
Seynt veuian " (Vivian) is termed " of Julyan " in the Cotton MS. I am not
aware that any Church of St Vivian exists in Rome.

Line 437. St Eusebius is here introduced as connected with the aforenamed Church of St Vivian. The Lambeth MS., however, line 554, speaks
of the Church of St Eusebius himself, which I presume to be correct ; but
the poem hereabouts in all the three MSS. is obviously a good deal muddled.
Compare l. 442 Vernon with l. 559 Lambeth.

Lines 463-4 are new in the Vernon MS. My old authority, Francino,
confirms the statement that a (daily) indulgence of 1000 years and Lents is to

be obtained at St Matthew's Church—to which he adds the remission of one-seventh of one's sins.

Lines 473-4. *The Church of St Anthony* is named in the Vernon MS. only, l. 473 having evidently slipped out of the Lambeth MS. by mischance. There are in Rome two Churches of St Anthony;—one near S^a Maria Maggiore and St Praxed's, with a Hospital; the other named Sant' Antonio de' Portoghesi, near La Scrofa, dedicated by Pope Gelasius to Sts Anthony and Vincent. To it are annexed a hospital for the Portuguese, and many indulgences and privileges for that nation. The particular grace mentioned by our poet, the remission of one-seventh of one's penance, is not, however, confirmed by Francino with regard to either of these churches.

Lines 529 to 532 set forth the indulgences attaching to S^a Maria Maggiore from Assumption-day to the feast of the Virgin's Nativity (15 August to 8 September). The Lambeth MS. says, Assumption-day to Christmas-day, which is an error.

Line 536. Here the name "Prudencian" is erroneous; it should be, as in the Lambeth MS., " Pudencyam "—St Pudentiana.

Line 548. The Vernon MS. reads " hostelled," instead of " harborowed," as in the Lambeth MS.; confirming the inference in my former notes that the statement applies " rather to the house of Pudens than to the cemetery."

Line 558. The extraordinary term "Emperour seint Antonine" seems to point to some corruption of the text. As observed in the former notes, the incident referred to could not, by comparison of dates, have happened in the reign of any of the Antonines.

Lines 563 to 568. *The Church of San Martino in Monte*, called also *San Silvestro e San Martino*, was built by Symmachus I. in A.D. 500, on the Esquiline Hill, upon the ruins of the Thermæ of Trajan, and was modernized in 1650. There had been an earlier church on the same spot, founded by S. Silvester in the time of Constantine. I know of no particular reason why the text should specify that the edifice " is not round." The text states that Popes Silvester and Leo are buried under the high altar. I do not find Leo named elsewhere ; Murray's Handbook mentions Silvester and Martin I., and Francino concurs in this statement, adding the names of three other Popes.

Lines 569 to 572. There is a Church of San Salvatore del Lauro which stands on the site of the laurel-grove near the Portico of Europa. It was founded in 1450, nearly a century later than the date of our Vernon MS., so that one cannot refer to this Church the allusion in the text. This is the only Church " of seint Saluator " known to me in Rome.

Line 601. Our present text seems to be correct in here naming " Seint Sabyne " (Sabinus), instead of the " Seint Sabasabyne " of the Lambeth MS.

Lines 609 to 612. *The Church of St Marcellus*, in the Corso, was built by a Roman lady in the 4th century, in honour of Pope St Marcellus, who, by order of Maxentius, was confined in this spot over a stable, the stench of which is alleged to have killed him. It was rebuilt in 1519 by Sansovino, the façade being of a later date. The ceremony of the Exaltation of the

Cross is held here on 14 September. Francino does not specify the 1000 years' indulgence of our text, but plenary remission on St Marcellus's day.

Lines 655-6 state that the good knight sometime named Placidas lies at the Church of St Eustace. In the Lambeth MS. the person thus named is St Eustace himself; and, as I can find out nothing about Placidas, I am disposed to infer that he and Eustace are one and the same person.

Line 664 clears up the difficulty in the corresponding line, 866, of the Lambeth MS., which states that "the Mawdlene" is in the Church of St Cecilia. We now learn that this is a foot of the Magdalene.

Line 680. *The Church of San Grisogono* (Chrysogonus), a saint who was martyred at Aquileia under Diocletian, is in the Trastevere, and supposed to date originally from the time of Constantine; rebuildings took place in 1129 and 1623. An Englishman may like to remember this church in connection with Archbishop Langton, who was its titular Cardinal. The 400 years' indulgence of our poem is not confirmed by Francino, but plenary remission on the day of St Chrysogonus.

Lines 681 to 688. I cannot clearly identify the "chirche of seint tyre and seint Ion;" but should suppose it to be not improbably *the Church of Sts John and Paul*. There are at least six other churches in Rome bearing the name of St John. The Church of Sts John and Paul—not the apostles, but martyrs of the reign of Julian—was built on the Cœlian Hill, in the 4th century, on the site of the house of these Saints.

Lines 693 to 696. "Seint Angel" may be either *the Church of Sant' Angelo in Bórgo*, or that of Sant' Angelo in Pescaria, close to the Portico of Octavius, and interesting in connection with the enterprise of Rienzi. I should rather suppose it to be the former church, which was built by a beatified Pope Gregory in consequence of his having seen the Archangel Michael sheathing his blood-stained sword above the citadel, or Mole of Hadrian. Francino does not name 1000 years' indulgence as applicable to either of these churches; but plenary remission, at the first, on the octave of St Michael, and, at the second, on the 18th July and 29th September.

Line 701. *The Church of St Adrian* is in the Forum, and is said to be the ancient Ærarium consecrated to this Saint by Pope Honorius.

Line 704. *The Church of St Clement*, between the Colosseum and the Lateran, is built over a still more ancient church, which was discovered in 1858, with results of great importance to Christian archæology; the upper church dates probably from the beginning of the 12th century. The traditional origin of the whole foundation was an oratory built by Clement the third Bishop of Rome, a fellow-labourer with St Paul. Instead of the 2000 years' indulgence of the text, Francino specifies plenary remission on the Monday following the second Sunday of Lent, as well as a daily indulgence of 40 years and Lents, doubled during Lent.

Line 705. The Church of "seint Steuene" is probably the Church of *santo stefano Rotondo*, on the Cœlian Hill, now generally supposed to have been originally the circular portion of the Macellum Grande, or Butchers'-

meat Market, erected in Nero's time. It was consecrated by Simplicius I. in A.D. 467, and restored by Nicholas V. towards 1447. Rome contains at least two other churches to St Stephen.

Lines 707 to 712 revert to the Church of "seint saluatour"; see l. 569. The "Bethleem" here mentioned is, I suppose, a Chapel of the Nativity.

Lines 717 to 719. I have been unable to trace the "*Chapel of vre ladi*" at which St Thomas of Canterbury kept school. It may be a separate building; or it may possibly be merely a chapel in the church last previously mentioned, that of St Alexius, which does, it seems, contain (as Francino relates it) "that image of the most blessed Virgin, on the high tabernacle, which used to be in the city of Edessa—before which the most blessed Alexius, being in the said city, often made prayer. And, going one day to the said church to pray, he found the doors closed; and the said image said twice to the porter, 'Open and give entrance to the Man of God, Alexius, who is worthy of heaven.'"

Lines 720 to 726. *The Church of St Urban,* here mentioned, does not appear in my authorities.

The last service I can tender for my reader's acceptance may be to refer him to a book bearing very closely upon the subject-matter of the "Stacions of Rome," and which I find thus entered in a Bookseller's catalogue:— "Mirabilia Romæ; a German Block-book of nearly 200 pages, being a Handbook for the Pilgrims at Rome in the 15th century. With the most curious descriptions of the relics kept in the Churches; among them the head of St Peter, milk of the Virgin, the circumcisions of Christ, &c.—and of the indulgences given by the priests of the various Churches. Small 4to; 12 copies only reprinted in facsimile by J. Ph. Berjeau." One regrets to read this last item, suggesting the small number of people that will ever be able to benefit by the reprint of so curious a book.

W. M. ROSSETTI.

P.S.—On the Porkington MS. I observe:

1. S. Sylvester in 1303, in connection with the heads of Peter and Paul, is a blunder.

2. S. Benyan's Church near S. Gellyan's. This Benyan is Julian in one MS. and Vivian in another: of Benyan I know nothing, but investigation might *possibly* bring something to light.

3. Placidas, the same person as Eustace: so I had guessed in writing on the Vernon MS.; and that conjecture may now be put positively.

The Stacions of Rome.

[Vernon MS., fol. 314, col. 3. The metrical points, and stops on each side of figures and after single letters, are those of the MS. Hyphens are put in by the Editor. The lines in the foot-notes refer to those of the Stacyons in *Political, Religious, & Love Poems*, pp. 113-44, E.E.T.Soc. 1866. C. stands for Cotton MS., Caligula A ii: L. for Lambeth MS. 306. This Vernon poem has been crossed through with the pen; also two lines have been drawn through the word *pope* in nearly every place where it occurs. The paragraph sign is alternately red and blue.]

HOse wole . his soule leche.
Lustne to me .I. wol him teche
Pardoun . Is þi soule bote.
4 At grete Rome . þer is þe Roote.   At Rome is the root of Pardon.
Pardoun . a word in frensch hit is.
Forȝiuenesse . of þi synnes i-wis.
¶ Þe Duchesse of troye . þat sum tyme was.
8 To Rome com . wiþ gret pres.
Of hire com Romilous . and Romilon.   Romilous and Romilon founded Rome.
Of whom . Rome furst bi-gon.
Heþene hit was . and cristned nouȝt.
12 Til petur . and poul . hit hedde I.-bouȝt.   Peter and Paul bought it with
Wiþ Gold . ne seluer . ne wiþ no goode.
Bot wiþ heore flesch . and with heore blode.   their blood.
For þei soffrede boþe dede.
16 Heore soule to saue . fro þe quede [1]

[1] The Cotton MS. inserts here lines 17-24, which the Lambeth MS. 306 follows the Vernon in omitting.

THE STACIONS OF ROME. (VERNON MS.)

At St Peter's

At seint peter . we schul bi-ginne.
to telle of pardoun . þat slakeþ sinne.
A feir Munstre . men mai þer se.

are 29 steps,
20 Niʒene and twenti greces þer be.
As ofte . as þou gost vp . Or doun.
Bi cause of deuocioun .

at each of which
þou schalt haue . at vche gre .
24 Mon . or Wommon . wheþer þou be.

you get 7 years' pardon.
Seuene ʒer . to pardoun
And þer-to godes benisoun.
¶ Pope Alisaundre hit graunted at Rome
28 To alle men . þat þider come.¹
In þat Munstre . men may fynde.

When the 100 Altars are blessed,
An hondred Auteres . bi-foren and be-hynde.
And whon þe Auters .I.-halewed wore.

you get 28 years' pardon and Lents,
32 xxviij² . ʒer . and so mony lentones more.
He ʒaf . and graunted . to pardoun.
And þer-to . godes benysoun.

There are 7 chief Altars, those of
¶ Among þe Auters . seuene þer be.
36 More of grace . and dignite.

I. the Vernicle,
¶ Þe Auter of þe vernicle is on.
Vp-on þe riht hond . as þou schalt gon .

II. Our Lady,
¶ Þe secunde . in þe honour of vr ladi is.

III. St Simon and Jude,
IV. St Andrew,
40 ¶ Þe þridde . of seint Symon and Jude I.-wis.
¶ Þe Feorþe . of seint Andreuʒ . þou schalt haue.

V. St Gregory,
¶ Þe Fifþe of seint gregori . þer he lyth in graue.

VI. St Leo,
¶ Þe Sixte . of seint leon þe pope.
44 Þer he song masse . in his Cope.

VII. Holy Cross.
¶ Of seint Crois . þat seuenþe is.
In wʒuche, no wommon schal comen I.-wis.³

At St. Peter's Altar
At þe Auter . þer peter is don.
48 Þe pope Gregori . ʒaf gret pardon.

¹ l. 37-44 inserted.   ² xxiiij Cotton MS., xviij Lambeth.
³ l. 63-6 inserted.

THE STACIONS OF ROME. (VERNON MS.) 3

	Of sunnes forʒete*n* . and oþes also.	
	xxviij . ʒer . he ʒaf þer to.	is 28 years' pardon,
	From holy þursday . In to la*m*masse	and daily from Holy Thursday to
52	Eueriche day . more and lasse.	Lammas
	¶ Þe*n*ne is xiiij þousend ʒer.	14,000 years.
	To alle þat come . to þat Mu*n*ster.	
	Of seint Martin . þ*a*t eiʒteþe day.¹	On the anni- versary of the
56	Þat Munstre was halwed . as I.ou say.	consecration of the Minster,
	Þe*n*ne is xiiijM ʒer . and lentones þer-to.	14,000 years, &c.
	Þe þridde p*ar*t . of þi penaunce vndo.	
	Whon þe vernicle schewed is.	When the Vernicle is
60	Gret p*ar*doun . forsoþe þer is . I.-wis	showed.
	Þreo þousend ʒer . as I. ow telle	[Fol. 514 b. col. 1. 3000 years to
	To Men þat in . þe Cite dwelle.	dwellers in the City,
	And men þat dwelle be sydeward.	9000 to dwellers near,
64	Nyne þousend ʒer . schal ben heore part.	
	¶ And þ*o*u þat passest ouer þe séé.	12,000 to those who cross the
	Twelue þousend ʒer . is graunted to þe.	sea.
	And þe*r*to . þow schalt winne more.	
68	Þe þr*i*dde part for-ʒiuenes . of al þi sore.	
	In lentone is . an holy grace.	In Lent all pardons are
	Vche p*ar*don is doubled . in þat place.²	doubled.
	To seint poul . as I. wene.	On the road to *St Paul's* is
72	Foure Myle is . holde bi-twene.	
	In þ*a*t wey . Is gret pardoun.	great pardon.
	And of mony sunnes . Remissiou*n*.	
	Saul was his name . be-foren.	(Saul was his name
76	Siþen the tyme . þat he was born.	
	Heþene he was . and cristnet nouʒt.	
	Til crist put hit . in his þouʒt.	
	¶ Þat holy Mon . Ananias.	till Ananias christened him
80	Him cristnet . þorw godes gras.	
	And cleped him Poul . petres broþer.	Paul.)
	For þe ton schulde . cu*m*forte þe toþer.	

¹ l. 75-7 instead of this.   ² l. 93-102 inserted.

4   THE STACIONS OF ROME.   (VERNON MS.)

On St. Paul's Conversion day is 100 years' pardon;
at his Festival 1000 years.

On Childermas-day, 4000 years,

and for a whole year's Sundays

as much pardon as for a pilgrimage to St James's.

At St Anastasius's,

daily,

7000 years' pardon

Pope Urban

forgives contrite men all their sins.

Silvester forgives pilgrims to this church

broken penance and oaths.

Outside is the stone on which St Paul was beheaded,

whence 3 wells sprung

that heal the sick.

    In þat ilke . conuercioun.
84 He ʒaf an hondred ʒer . to pardoun.
    And at þe feste . of his day.
    A þousend ʒer . haue þou may.
    ¶ On childermasse day . In cristemasse
88 Is foure þousend ʒer . to more and lasse.[1]
    And ʒif þou beo þere . al þe ʒer.
    Vche sunday . in þat munster
    þou shalt haue . as muche pardoun.
92 As þou to seint Jame . went and com.
    HEr may we . not longe be
    To seint Anastace . moste we.
    Two Myle . is holde be-twene.
96 Of feir wey . and of grene.
    Vche day . ʒif þou wolt craue.
    Seuen þousent ʒer . þer may þou haue[2]
    Pope Vrban . þat holy syre.
100 So rewardede . men heore huyre
    Men þat ben schriuen . and verrey contrit.
    Of alle heore synnes . god [3] makeþ heom quit.
    ¶ Pope Siluestre . to pilgrimes.
104 þat þider comeþ . diuerse tymes.
    Penaunce broken . and oþes also.
    His oune helpe . he putte þerto.
    Wrapping of Fader . or Moder . ʒif hit be
108 In godes nome . he forʒiueþ þe.[4]
    Bi-fore þe dore . stont a ston.
    Seynt poules hed . was leyd þeron.
    A traitur . smot of his heued.
112 Wiþ a swerd . þer hit was leued.
    þer aftur spronge welles þre.
    Hose is þere . wel may he se.
    Of water . boþe feir and gode
116 Men . and Wimmen . han had heore bote

[1] l. 121-4 inserted.   [2] l. 135-6 inserted.
[3] Cott. he [Pope Urban]   [4] l. 147-8 inserted.

THE STACIONS OF ROME. (VERNON MS.).

    IN þat place . a Chapel is.
    Scala celi . clepet hit is.   *Scala Cœli* is there, Our Lady's second Chapel.
    Laddere of heuene men clepeþ hitte.
120 In þe honour of vr ladi . be my witte
    þat is þe secou*n*de chapel . of here.
    þat men in Roome . tellen þere.
    Mony is . þat holy bone.
124 þat vnder þe heiȝe Auter is done.
    Ten þousend Martyres . w*it*h honour.   10,000 Martyrs died there in Tiberian's reign.
    In tyme of Tibian[1] . þe Empe*r*our.
    þei suffrede deþ . alle in Rome.
128 Heore soules in heuene for to come.
    þer men may helpe . quike . and dede   Prayer there helps both quick and dead.
    As þe clerkes . in bokes rede [2]
    Foure and fourti popes . g*r*anted þan.
132 þat liggen . at seint Sebastian.
    Pope Vrban . Siluestre . and Benet.
    Leon . Clement . confermede hit.

    Nou passe we forþ . in vre gate
136 To seinte Marie . þe Nunciate   To *St Mary the Nunciate's* is 2 long miles.
    Two Mile is bitwene . I. vnder-sto*n*de.
    But þi aren . sumdel longe.
    þer is writen . as I. ow say.
140 Of vre ladi . in þat way.   [Fol. 314 b. col. 2.] Our Lady promised to save from hell-fire sinners who came there.
    A-doun heo com wiþ Angeles.
    To a Frere of þat hous.
    And seide to þat ilke mon.
144 þat out of dedly sy*n*ne . þider com.'
    Fro þe fuir of helle . heo wolde hi*m* schilde.
    As heo was Mayden . and moder Mylde [3].

    TO Fabian and Bastian . passe we   To *St Fabian and Bastian's* is 3 miles.
148 þider we haue . Myles þre
    An Angel fro*m* heuene . a-dou*n* com.   An Angel told
    To seint Gregor . þat holy mon.   St Gregory

[1] ? For Tibe*r*ian   [2] l. 171-9 inserted.   [3] l. 195-8 inserted.

6   THE STACIONS OF ROME. (VERNON MS.)

	As he song masse . atte hei3e Auter.
152	Of seint Sebastian . þat holy Marteer.
	And seide here . in þis place.
that remission of sins was there.	Is li3t of heuene . bi godes grace
	þer is . of mony sunnes . remissioun
Pope Gelasius gave 40 years pardon too.	156	And Fourti 3er . to pardoun
	And also monye lentones mo.
	Pope Gelasius . 3af þer to.
This Church has as much pardon as St Peter's	As muche pardoun . is þere.
160	So is . in seint peteres Munstere.
on account of the holy bones that	Be þe enchesun . of þe holy bones.
	Þat þere . weore buried at ones.
lay under-ground 100 years.	And þere lay . ¹ vnder grounde
164	An hundred 3er . er þei weore founde
	Afturward . þorw godes grace
	Þei weore founden . In þat place
	And worschuped . with gret Solempnite²
168	As þei ou3te for to be.

Each of six Popes OF sixe popes . tellen I. wile³
On aftur oþur . as hit is skile.
Pope Pelagius . I. telle þe.
172 Gregor . and Siluester . þer beoþ þre.
Alisaundre . and Nichole . þer beoþ fyue.
Honorius þe sixte . while he was on lyue
gave 1000 years' pardon to all there shriven clean of mortal sin. Vche of hem . 3af his grace.
176 A þousend 3er . in that place
To alle þat euere . þat þer beone.
And of dedly sunnes be clene.
For elles may þi soule . not lyue.
180 Bot of dedly sunnes . þou be schriue.

---

¹ Cotton MS. inserts 'petur & powle,' and makes the 'an' of next line 'Fyfe.'
² This line is omitted in the Cotton MS.
³ This line is erased by a later hand in the Vernon MS. C. puts l. 171 here before l. 169.

THE STACIONS OF ROME. (VERNON MS.) 7

    A lutel be-hynde . þou maiʒt go.   *Behind is an under-ground*
    Þer stont a Chapel . in a wro.   *Chapel where 44 martyr-Popes*
    Foure and fourti popes . sum time were.   *lived,*
184 verrey Martirs . þat liueden þere.
    vche of hem . ʒaf his benisoun.
    For þer is plener remissioun[1].   *and there is full remission of all*
    Of alle þe sunnes . þou hast I.-don.   *sins,*
188 Sin þou in þis world . coom.
    Al is . for-ʒeuen þe.
    So I . herde of clerkes . put þer han be.
    And ʒif þow dye . þiderward.   *and heaven's bliss if you die thither-*
192 Heuene blisse . schal ben þi part.   *ward.*
    But þou most take . Candel liht[2].   *(You must take a*
    Elles þou gost . Merk as niht[2].   *candle*
    For vnder þe eorþe . most þou wende.   *and go under-ground to the*
196 Þow maiʒt not seo . bi-fore ne bi-hynde.   *Chapel.*
    For þider fledde Mony men.   *Martyrs fled there*
    For drede of deþ . to sauen hem.   *for refuge)*
    And suffrede peynes . harde and sore.
200 In heuene to dwelle . for euer more

    Nou wende we . to þe palmalle.   *At the Palmalle (or footsole) called*
    domine quo uadis . men hit calle   *Domine, quo vadis ? where*
    Þer Peter mette with Ihesu.   *Peter met Jesus,*
204 And seide lord . whoder woltou.
    Crist onswerde . to peter þo
    In to Rome . he seide I. go.
    Eft to dye . on Rode for þe
208 Þou dredest to dye . peter for me.
    Lord he seide . Merci I. crie.
    To take my deþ .I. am redie.
    Þer is a signe . of his foot.   *and a mark of Christ's foot is left*
212 On Marbel ston . þer he stod.   *on the marble,*
    Vche day . two þousent ʒer   *is daily 2000 years'*
    Of pardoun . þou mai haue þer.   *pardon,*

        [1] C. omits this line.
    [2-2] C. transposes and slightly alters these lines.

and remission of all sins.		þer is writen on a ston . gret pardoun
	216	þer is of alle sunes . Remissioun [1].
At St Thomas's,		**A**t seint thomas þe Apostle of Inde.
		a chirche i-wis . þou mai þer fynde
the giving of alms		put þin hond . with almes dede
	220	And þou schalt haue . þer gret mede
will gain you the prayers of men in the Holy Land,		To helpe hem . þat ben þere.
		In þe holi lond . or elles where.
		Niht and day . to preye for þe.
	224	For help of þi charite.
		Of moni popes . þat þer han bene.
		þis pardoun to þe . is graunted clene.
and 14,000 years' pardon, &c.		Fourtene þousend ȝer . and sum del more
	228	þe þridde part forȝiuenesse . of þi sore.
Stations get you great pardon.		And pardon in Rome . þat is grete.
		þe Stacions . þer men hit clepe
		Pope Bonefas . confermed alle.
	232	For euer more . lasten hit schalle.
At St John Lateran		**T**o seint Ion lateran . moste we.
		A while þere . for to be.
is as much pardon as anywhere in Rome.		To telle of pardoun . þat is þore.
	236	For in al Rome . ne is no more.
		þen þer is graunted . of Ihesu crist.
		þorw preyer of seint Ion þe Ewangelist.
		And seint Ion Baptist also.
	240	To alle . þat þider wol go.
For formerly an Emperor,		¶ For sum tyme was . an Emperour.
		þat liuede in Rome . with gret honour.
Constantine,		Kyng Costantyn . men dude him calle
	244	Boþe in boure . and eke in halle.
		In Mahoun . was al his þouht.
believed in Mahoun,		For in crist . ne leeuede he nouht.
		A . Mesel forsoþe . we fynde he was.
and was a leper,	248	Til crist sende him . of his gras.

[1] C. l. 268-77 inserted, about St John of the Latin gate.

¶ Pope Siluestre . gon him preche. — till Pope Silvester
Cristes lawes . forte teche.
So leeuede he wel . In godes sone. — converted and
252 And cristene mon . wolde he bi-come.
He dude him cristne . as I. ou telle — christened him.
In þis Miracle . þus hit bi-felle
Þat þe water wesch . a-wey his sinne — The water washed away his sins and
256 And al þe fulþe . þat he was Inne. — disease,
¶ Þenne spak þe Emperour. — and he
To pope siluestre with gret honour.
Siluestre he seide . godes clerke. — acknowledged
260 I. mai seo nou . þat er was derke.
Mi misbileue . haþ blyndet me. — his misbelief,
Þat I . mihte . þe [soþe¹] not se.
Of godes mihtes . ne of his werkes.
264 I. wol bi-comen . on of his clerkes.
Mi paleys I ȝiue hit . to þin honde. — gave up his palace to be
Of me þou schalt hit vnderfonge
And mak þer-of . godes hous. — God's House,
268 For I. wole . þat hit beo þous.
I. wol him loue . with al mihtes.
And preie him to ben . on of his knihtes.
And whon þou hast . so I.-do. — and asked Silvester to bless all
272 Ȝif þi benyson . þer-to. — worshippers there.
To alle hem . þat þider come.
To honoure . godes sone.
And seint Jon . þe Ewangelyst.
276 Peter and poul . and seint Jon þe Baptist.

Pope siluester . þenne seide he. — Silvester promised them
Of peter and poul . and of me
Þei schal be clene . of synne and pyn.
280 As crist clanset . þe of þyn.
And as þe fulþe . fel fro þe.
So clene of sunne . schal þei be.

¹ C. inserts mote, and L. soothe.

10   THE STACIONS OF ROME. (VERNON MS.)

cleansing from all sin.

Of alle maner clansyng of synne.
284 þat non schal dwellen . heore soule with-inne
     ¶ Pope Bonefas . telleþ þis tale

If men did but know the pardon to be had at Rome,

¹ʒif men wuste . grete and smale
þe pardoun þat is . at grete Rome.
288 þei wolde tellen . In heore dome.¹

they'd not go

Hit were no neod . to mon in cristiante

to the Holy Land or St Catherine's;

To passe in to þe holy lond . ouer þe séé.²
To Jerusalem . ne to kateryne.
292 To bringe monnes soule . out of pyne

for in Rome is pardon without end ; and

For pardoun þer is . with-outen ende.
Wel is him . þat þider may wende ³

Relics too—

Rerikes þer beo . monyon
296 In worschupe of crist . and seynt Ion.
In þe Rof . ouer þe popes se.

I. A Saviour, not painted by man ;

A saluatour . þer may þou se
Neuer I.-peynted . with hond of Mon.
300 As men I. Roome . tellen con.

[Fol. 315, col. 1.]

Whon Seluestre halwed þat place.
Hit apeered þer . þorw godes grace.
     ¶ ⁴ Anoþer chapel is . in þat hous.
304 þer-Inne beoþ Relikes . precious.⁴

II. The Table of the Last Supper ;

þe Table . þer men may se.
þat crist made . on his maunde
On scherþorsday . whon he brak bred.
308 Bi-fore þe tyme . þat he was ded.
Eteþ of þis . hit doþ ʒow good.
Hit is my flesch . and my blod.
Whon ʒe schul me . here not fynde.
312 Hit schal ʒou kepen . from þe feende.

---

¹⁻¹ For these three lines C. has one, l. 349, 'And y tell ythe forth with-outene fayle.'
² See the poem at the end of this about the miseries of the Pilgrim's sea-sickness.
³ l. 356-71 inserted.
⁴⁻⁴ Omitted by C., see l. 380 : L. has them.

¶ [1] A-bouen an Auter . is maked of tre.
Is a table I. telle þe
Vnder þat auter . In a whucche is done.   III. In a hutch

316 Wiþ holy Relikes . monione.[1]
¶ Two tables þer is .I. vnderstonde.   the Two Tables of the Law given
Þat crist wrott on . with his honde.   to Moses;
And tok þe lawe . to Moyses.
320 His folk to kepen . in godes pes.
¶ Þe ȝerde of AAron . þat was good.   IV. Aaron's rod;
Hit turned watur . in-to blod.
And from blod . to water a-ȝen
324 To schewe . þat þei weore gode men.
¶ Angel mete . men seiþ þer is.   V. Angels' food (Manna);
And of the bones . and þe fisch.   VI. Parts of the(?) Loaves and Fishes
·Þat crist fedde . fiue þousend men.   that fed 5000 men, and of the
328 And Relef lafte . aftur hem.[2]   Fragments;
¶ Þer beoþ cloþes . of Ihesu crist.   VII. Christ's clothes;
And askes . of seint Ion þe Babtist.   VIII. John the Baptist's ashes;
And þe cloþ . þat crist gon wiþ him lede   IX The table-cloth of the Last
332 On scherþorsday . his disciples with to fede.   Supper;
¶ [3] And þe cloþ . þat crist was wounden Inne   X. Christ's swaddling cloth;
Whon he was child . for monnes sinne.[3]
¶ Of Blod . and Watur . þer is also.   XI. Blood and Water from
336 Þat out of cristes sydes . gan go.[4]   Christ's side;
¶ And of his Flesch . þat circumcise   XII. Christ's foreskin, &c., &c.
Men hit holden . in gret a prise.[5]
And oþer Relikes moni on.
340 In worschupe of crist . and seint Ion.

H ere mai we . no lengore be.
In to þe popes halle . moste we.·   In the *Pope's Hall*
In þat halle . þre dores þer be.   are three doors;
344 Vche day open . ȝe may hem se

[1-1] Omitted by C.—see l. 388—not by L.
[2] C. transposes this and the line above, and inserts after it l. 400-15, about the four Pillars of Brass, and St John's Chains.
[3] C. alters these; see l. 426-7.   [4] C. inserts l. 424-5.
[5] C. inserts l. 430-7.

passing through them gives		As often as þou passest . þorw eny of hem. And entrest . þorw a-noþer þen. And passest þorw a-noþer . of hem þre.
40 years' pardon.	348	Fourti ӡer . is graunted to þe.[1]
In Sancta Sanctorum is a figure		**N**ou passe we . to sancta sanctorum. þat is þe Chapel . of Clericorum.[2]
of the Saviour		þer Inne is . þe saluatour.
	352	To whom men doþ . gret honour.
sent to Our Lady from heaven		þe whuche was sent . to vre ludi. Whon heo was . in eorþe vs bi.
by Christ;		From hire sone . þat is a-boue.
	356	After þe tyme . of his Assencione.[3]
and the heads of Peter and Paul		¶ Of Peter . and Poul . heore hedes ben þere. Wel I.-closed . vnder þe heiӡe Autere. And oþer Relikes . mony on.
locked in a stone,	360	þer ben closed in a ston.
of which the Pope keeps the keys.		¶ Hose is þer . pope of Rome þe keyes with him . he haþ I.-nome þat no mon may hem þer I.-seo.
	364	Bot he him self . present beo.
Full remission is to be had there.		In þat chapel . ӡif þou wolt craue Plener remissioun . þou maiӡt haue.
At *Holy Rood Church* is a Chapel		**A**t þe chirche . of þe holy Roode.
	368	Is a chapel . feir and gode.[4]
that Constance built.		Constance . þat holi wommon. Of kyng Constantyn . heo com. His douӡter heo was . and þat is scene.
	372	For þorw preyer . of seynt Elene. þat holy place . heo made þus. In þe honour . of þat holy crois.
Silvester granted		Pope Siluestre . hit halewed þo
	376	And gret pardoun . he ӡaf þer-to

[1] C. inserts l. 448—461.
[2] C. has 'In þat chapelle shalle no womon come,' l. 463, p. 130.
[3] C. alters the next eight lines; see l. 470-6, p. 130.
[4] C. inserts l. 480-1, p. 130-1.

THE STACIONS OF ROME. (VERNON MS.) 13

  Vche Sonenday . in þe ʒer. *it 250 years'*
  And Wednesday . ʒif þou beo þer. *pardon every Sunday and Wednesday,*
  Of pardoun two hundred . and fifti [1] ʒer.
380 And eueri day . an hundred is þer. *and 100 every other day.*
  And a sponge of galle . and Eysel. *Its Relics are—*
  Of þat venym . is þer gret del.[2] *I. The Sponge of Gall and Vinegar*
  þat Jewes profred him . to drinke þo *offered to Christ on the Cross;*
384 Whon he seide . Ciscio.
  And a nayl . whon Crist Ihesu was. *II. A nail he was crucified with;*
  Don on Rode tre . for vre trespas.
  ¶ In þat Chirche . is also *III. A piece of the Penitent Thief's Cross;*
388 Of þe Croys . he was on do.
  þat heng on Rode . him by.[3]
  And of his sunnes . hedde Merci.
  And a Titil . of sire pilat. *IV. Pilate's Writing,*
392 þei may hit rede . þat beo þerat.
  þis is Ihesu . of Nazareth. *"This is Jesus the King of the Jews."*
  Kyng of Iewes . þat þolede deth.
  þat titel is hud . hit wol not ley.
396 In A Croys . þat hongeþ hey.
  In þe Maner . of a bouwe.
  In mideward þe chirche rof .I. trouwe.
  In þat maner . hit is do.
400 For no mon schulde come þer to.

  Of more pardoun .I. wol ʒou say.
  At seint Laurence . vche a day. *At St Lawrence's daily is 7000 years' pardon, &c.,*
  Seuen þousend ʒer . with lentons þer-to.
404 And pridde part . of þi penaunce vndo.
  Pope pelagius . þat holy mon.
  þat chirche . halewen he bi-gon.
  And graunted al þat pardoun.
408 And þer-to . his Benisoun.[4]

---

[1] C. two thousand and fyfe.
[2] C. substitutes 'Relykes þer be mony & fele,' l. 494, p. 131, for this, and puts it before l. 401 here.
[3] C. makes it Christ's cross and the Thief's : l. 501-3, p. 132.
[4] C. inserts l. 522-31, p. 132-3.

14 THE STACIONS OF ROME. (VERNON MS.)

and, for a year of Wednesdays, power to free a soul from Purgatory.

And ȝif þow be þere . al þe ȝer.
Vche Wednesday . in þat munster.
Þenne hastou . of crist pouweer.
412 A. soule to drawe . from purgatori fer.

At St Simplicius' Faustine and Beatrice

At seint symple faustin . and beatris.
Þat were verray Martirs . of pris.
Seint symple . pope of Rome he was.
416 God him sente . a wel feir gras.

are 7000 holy bones,

Vij þousende [1] holy bones.
He gedered to-gedere . but not at ones.
In his chirche . he dude hem graue.
420 He was siker . heore soules to saue.

and all men shriven there get

And ȝaf pardoun . to alle þo.
Þat ben schriuen . and þider wol go.

7000 years' pardon and more.

Seue [2] þousend ȝer of pardoun . and more.
424 In þe honour of hem . þat liggen þore.[3]
Whon he was ded . þer was he graue
Crist his soule . mote saue.

At St Vivian's

At þe chirche . of seynt veuian.
428 Hit is writen . on a ston.

are 3000 martyrs buried,

Þat þre þousend Martirs ben bured þare.
Crist leue here soules . wel to fare.
Honorius . þat holy pope.
432 Þat chirche he halewed . in his cope.

and the pardon is 7000 years.

Seue þousend ȝer . of pardoun.
He ȝaf . [4] at þat processyoun.
To laste for euere more.[4]
436 To hem þat come þore.
¶ In þat churche . is an holy prest.
Þat deore is . wiþ Ihesu Crist.

At St Eusebius's

Eusebius . was his name
440 To tellen of him . hit is no blame

[1] C. Seuen hondred, l. 540. [2] C. Fyfe.
[3] C. omits the two next lines, and puts Iulyan for vcuian, in l. 447.
[4-4] C. omits, and ends at l. 456 here ; l. 553, p. 134, *Pol., Rel., & Love Poems.*

THE STACIONS OF ROME. (VERNON MS.) 15

     Hit is writen . in a ston.
     I. wol ȝou telle . or ȝe gon.
     Pope Gregori . þer he dude stonde
444 þe churche he halewed . with his honde.
     And ȝaf pardoun . as I. ow say.   *is 100 years and 50 days' pardon,*
     An hundred ȝer . and fifti day.
     And þreo ȝer more . I. ow telle.   *and 3 years more to abate hell's*
448 Forte Abate . þe peynes of helle.   *pains.*

     At þᵉ chirche . per seint Iulian lith.   *At St Julian's*
     Þer is his chin . with his teth.
     And oþer Relikes . mony and dere
452 To hem is graunted . Eiȝte þousend ȝere   *is 8000 years' pardon.*

     A noþur chirche . ȝit þer is.   *At St Matthew's*
     Of seint Matheu . men seyn hit is.
     In þe wei . as þou schalt gon.
456 To þe Churche . of seint Ion.
     Þer is an holy Arm . wel I.-diht.   *(where St Christopher's arm is,*
     Of seint Cristofre . Godes kniht.   *that Christ stood*
     In þat chirche . hit is do.
460 And gret pardoun . is graunted þer to.
     For crist him selue per-onne stod.
     Whon Cristofre him bar . ouer þe flod.
     Þer is a þousend ȝer . withouten mo.
464 And as mony lentones þer to.   *on) is 1000 years' pardon, &c.*

     IN þe Churche . of Viti . and Modesti   *At St Vitus and Modestus*
     Þer mowe ȝe sitte and resti.
     Þer is for-ȝeuen . þe pridde part of þi sinne   *a third of your sins are forgiven,*
468 What tyme þou comest . þe chirche with-inne
     Seue þousend Martirs . ben buried þere   *7000 Martyrs are buried there.*
     As hit is writen . in þat Munstere.
     In tyme of þe Emperour . Antony.
472 Hit is writen þer apertely[1].

     IN þe Churche . of seint Anton[1]   *At St Anthony's, one-seventh of*
     Is seueþe part . þi penaunce vndon.   *your penance excused.*

[11] For these lines L. has one, l. 589, 'that tyrant was, and paynyme.'

16 THE STACIONS OF ROME. (VERNON MS.)

At *St Mary the Major*	At seinte Marie . þe maiour.
	476 Þer is a chirche . of gret honour.
	At þe heiȝe Auter . hit is seid.
lie St Matthew	Þat þe bodi of seint Matheu . is leid.
and St Jerome,	And the bodi . of seint Jerom¹.
	480 An holy doctor . he was on¹.
	From þe Cite . of Damas.
	He was brouȝt . in to þat plas.
before a chapel called Presepe (boards from the Manger of the Nativity).	Bi-foren a chapel . he was pit.
	484 Presepe . men clepeþ hit.
	Vppon his graue . lith a ston.
	And a Crois . is graue þer on.
	Aboue þe ston . a gredyl is.
	488 Of Iren strong .I. wot hit is.
Its Relics are—	And Relikes þer ben . mony one².
	In honur . of vr ladi . and hire sone².
I. The Cloth Christ was put in when He was born;	¶ A luytel cloþ . þer is þer-to.
	492 In whuche cristes bodi . was furst in i-do
	Of his Moder . whon he was born
	To saue þe world . þat was for-lorn³.
II. The Hay He lay on before the Ass;	¶ And of þat heiȝ . more and lasse.
	496 Þat crist lay on . bi-fore þe Asse.
III. An Arm of St Thomas a Becket;	¶ And an Arm . men seyn is þer.
	Of seint Thomas þe holy Marter.
IV. Part of his brain;	And a parti of þe brayn.
	500 At Canterburi . he was slayn.
V. His Rochet;	¶ And a Rochet þat is good.
	Al be-spreint . with his blod.
	Wheche he hedde on . whon he was take.
	504 For al holi churche sake.
VI. An Image of Our Lady,	¶ And an ymage . sikerly.
	Wonder feir . of vre ladi.

¹⁻¹ L. varies ; see l. 595-6, p. 135.
²⁻² For these lines L. has l. 605-8, p. 136.
³ L. inserts l. 613-14 (about Christ's foreskin).

THE STACIONS OF ROME. (VERNON MS.) 17

¶ Seint Luik . while he lyuede in londe.   which St. Luke meant to have painted,
508 Wolde haue peynted hit . wit*h* his ho*n*de
    And whon he hedde . ordeyned so.
    Alle colours . þat schulde þer to.
    He fond an ymage . al a-pert.   but one done by Angels' hands was put in its place.
512 Non such þer was . middelert.
    Mad wit*h* Angel hond . and not wit*h* his.
    As men in Rome . witnesseþ þis.
    And writen hit is al þere
516 On a table . atte heiȝe Autere
    Pardou*n* þer is . þat men may se.
    Grau*n*ted of popes . þat þer han be.
    Vppon eue*r*i chirche haly day   On every Church Holy Day is 1000 years' pardon,
520 A þousend ȝer . þer haue þou may.
    And þer to . þou schalt haue more.
    Forȝiuenesse . of al þi sore.[1]   forgiveness of sorrows, and 800 years' more pardon.
    And eiȝte[2] hundred ȝer þer to.
524 Wel is him . þat þider may go.
    In eue*r*i feste . of vre ladi.   At every Feast of Our Lady
    Þerto graunted . seint Gregori.
    An hundred ȝer . to pa*r*doun.   100 years' pardon.
528 And þe*r*to godes Benysou*n*.
¶ In vre lauedi . þe Assu*m*pcion,   From the Assumption of the Virgin
    Þenne is þere . gret pa*r*dou*n*.
    In to þe day . þat heo[3] was born.   to her Birthday
532 Neuer a day . schal beo for-lorn.
    In þat tyme . þer is fourtene þousend ȝer.   is 14000 years' pardon.
    To alle þat come . to þat Munster.
    A Chirche . ȝit þer is.
536 Prudencian . clepet hit is.[4]   At *St Prudencian's*
    For-ȝiuenesse . of al þi synne
    At þat place . þer may þou winne.
    Seint Gregori . telleþ þus.
540 In þat place . and in þat hous.

[1] Altered in L. l. 624, p. 137.   [2] vii L.   [3] L. tyll*e* Ihes*u*.
[4] L. inserts l. 657-8, p. 137 here, alters the two next lines, and adds two, l. 661-2, about St Preselle's churchyard, after them.

18 THE STACIONS OF ROME. (VERNON MS.)

[Fol. 315 b. col. 1.]
are buried
4000 people:
and for every
body mentioned
by

pilgrims, they
get 1000 years'
pardon.

At *St Praxed's*

1300 martyrs

are buried.

Pope Innocent
granted every
man
1000 years'
pardon, &c.

At *St Martin's in
the Mount*

lie Popes Sil-
vester and Leo,

and 800 saints,

800 years' pardon.

At *St Saviour's*

1000 years'
pardon.

Ben buried þer .I. vnderstonde.
Fourti¹ þousend. of diuerse londe.
For eueri bodi . þow wolt of spelle
544 Hit is writen . as I. ow telle.
Þorw preyere of hem . þat þer be.
Þis pardoun . is graunted to þe
For Peter and poul . þat sum tyme were
548 Boþe þei weoren . hostelled þere
Þerfore alle pilgrimes . þat come þore.²
Hem is graunted a þousend ȝer . to hele her sore.²

At seint praxede . þat holy wommon.
552 riht þe soþe . tellen I. con.
A þousend bodies . with-outen mo.
And þreo hundred . ȝit þerto.
In þat place . buried þei be.
556 Heore soules with god . in dignite
Þer suffrede deþ . in his tyme.
Emperour . seint Antonine.
Pope Innocent . after þan.
560 Þer be graunted . to eueri man.
A þousend ȝer³ . to pardoun.
And þridde part . þi sinnes remissioun.

⁴At seint Martin . in þe mount.
564 Þer stont a chirche . is not round.
Vnder þe heie Auter . liþ seluester . and . leone
Þat weore popes . boþe in Rome
With oþere seyntes . monye I.-fere
568 Eiȝte hundred at ones . and as fele ȝere.

In þat wei . a Chirche þer is.
Of seint Saluatur .I. wot hit is.
Whon þou comest þer . þou maiȝt haue
572 A þousend ȝer . ȝif þou wolt craue

¹ L. *thre*, and alters the two next lines.
² L. omits these lines, but inserts 1. 673-84, on *Titulus Pastoris*.
³ L. 'O yere and xl dayes.'
⁴ For the ten next lines L. has l. 697—702, p. 138.

THE STACIONS OF ROME. (VERNON MS.) 19

<blockquote>
Another day in þe ȝer.
Of Seint peter . þe holy Marter.
A vincula . in þat londe
576 Lammasse day .I. vnderstonde.¹
For in þat day . is gret pardoun.
For þer is plener . remissioun.
And eueri day . ȝif þou wolt craue
580 Fyfe hundred ȝer . þer maiȝt þou haue
And as mony lentones mo
Pope gelasius . ȝaf þer to.
² þe Cheynes þere . meṇ may se.
584 Sikerliche .I. telle þe
þer peter was bounden . sikerly.
While he was . in eorþe vs by.

To a noþer . moste we go.
588 þere Apostles . liggen two
Crist vs kepe alle from wo
preyeþ alle . þat hit beo so.³
Furst with Costantyn . hit was set.
592 And siþen with heretykes . doun I.-bet
Pelagius . and pope Ion.
þei duden hit maken vp anon.
And ȝaf þer to . pardoun gret.
596 To alle þat þider comeþ . be stret.⁴
For þer is . mony a noble seinte
þer þei liggen . and not beon peynte³
¶ Seint Jacob . and seint philip liþ in schrine
600 And mony a noþer ⁵ . holy virgine
And seint Sabyne . writen we fynde
And a Tabart . of seint Thomas of Inde ⁶
Two þousend ȝer . þer may þou haue
604 þi soule hit mai . from helle saue
</blockquote>

On the day of St Peter ad Vincula;
(Lammas Day,)
is full remission,
and 500 years' pardon, and Lents.

The Church of The Holy Apostles
was first built by Constantine.

Many Saints lie there:
St James, St Philip, and
St Sabyne; also St Thomas's Tabard.
The pardon is 2000 years,

¹ L. inserts l. 707-8, p. 139.
² For the next five lines L. has l. 715-23, on the Relics.
³ L. omits this line.   ⁴ L. omits these lines.
⁵ L. Sent Eugenie þe.   ⁶ L. inserts l. 736-7, p. 139.

		And vche day . whon þou comest þare.
		þou mai3t deliuere . a soule from care.
doubled every Apostle's Day.		And on vche apostles . day.
	608	þis pardoun is doubled . as I. ow say.
At *St Marcelle's* is 1000 years' pardon.		¹**A** pousend 3er . þou mai3t telle
		At þe chirche . of seint Marcelle
		þat was sum tyme . pope of Rome
	612	For holi chirche . he soffrede Martirdome.¹
At *St Mary the Round*,		At seinte Marie . þe Rounde
		þer stont a chirche . on þe grounde
		þer is writen . as I. ow say.
on May 13, All Saints Day,	616	þat . at . þe prettenepe day . of may.²
		At al halewe day . whon hit i-come ²
is full remission.		þer is plener . Remissione ³
Agrippa built it for Sibyl's and Neptane's sake,	620	A.-Grippa . dude hit make.
		For Sibyl . and Neptanes . sake.
[Fol. 315 b. col. 2.]		Modres þei weren of corsede men.
		False fendes . ladden heom.
and called it *Pantheon,*		He 3af hit name . panteon.
	624	In al Rome . was such non.
made an image of gold,		A vigour he made . of gold rede.
		More þen God . he dude hit drede.
		Whon hit . in þe temple sat.
	628	Hit loked forþ . as a Cat.
called it Neptan,		He called hit Neptan . aftur his a-vys.
		He leeuede þer on . he was not wys⁴
put a cover of brass on its head, which was blown to St Peter's,	632	Vppon his heued . a couert of Bras.
		To seynte petres . blowen hit was.
		With a wynt of helle . as I. trouwe
		For no mon mihte hit . þider haue þrowe.
		þer hit stont I. telle þe.

---

¹⁻¹ L. has l. 742-5, p. 140, about St. Bartholomew's, given l. 711-12, p. 22, here.
² L. alters these lines.   ³ L. inserts 752-3.
⁴ L. puts l. 649 before l. 648, and inserts two (l. 766-7, p. 140) after the latter.

THE STACIONS OF ROME. (VERNON MS.)   21

636 ȝif þou go þider . þou may hit se.¹   *and there you may see it.*
 Þ At holy pope . Bonefas.   *Pope Boniface*
  Was folfuld . of Godes gras²
  To þe Emperour . soone he cam.
640 Julius . A wel good man.   *asked the Emperor Julian for the Pantheon,*
  Þat Temple he seide . þou ȝeue hit me
  I. preye hit þe . for Charite.³
  I. ȝeue hit þe . he seide . for euermore   *got it,*
644 In Amendement . of my sore.
  Þe Furste day . of Nouembre.   *and on November 1*
  Pope Bonefas . wiþ herte tendre.
  Þe folk of Rome . he gan to calle
648 And made hem semble . in þat halle
  He gedered hem to-gedere . alle in-same
  For þei wolde chaunge . þe halles name   *changed its name to*
  In þe honour . of vre ladi.
652 And alle þe seintes . þat sit hire bi.
  ⁴ Þis halle schal hette . seinte Mari rounde   *St Mary the Round.*
  He chaunged þe nome . in þat stounde

 At seint Eustas . lihþ a good kniht.   *At St Eustace's.*
656 Placidas . sum tyme he heiht.   *Placidas, his wife, and sons, lie.*
  He and his wif . and his twei sones I-fere
  liggen buried . vnder þe heiȝe Autere.
  Vche day . two þousend ȝer.   *Pardon daily, 2000 years.*
660 Pope Siluestre graunted þer.
  ⁵ **A**t seint saluatour . is writen openly.   *At St Salvadore, 1030 years' pardon.*
  A. þousend ȝer . and þritti⁵.
  At seint Celcy . is an hundred ȝer.   *At St Cecilia's is a foot of Mary Magdalene.*
664 A. fot of Marie Magdaleyn . is þer⁶.

¹ L. inserts l. 773-4, p. 140-1.   ² L. inserts l. 778-9, p. 141.
³ L. inserts l. 784-5, and alters the two next lines here.
⁴ L. alters the two next lines, and inserts l. 798, &c., here, and gives St Eustace's, altered at l. 850-55, p. 143. What follows l. 810 L., is represented here by l. 685-8, p. 22.
⁵⁻⁵ L. has l. 856-63, p. 143.
⁶ L. has first, l. 832-3, p. 142, and secondly, l. 864-7, p. 143.

22   THE STACIONS OF ROME. (VERNON MS.)

At St Mary Transpontine, 300 years' pardon.

¹ And þre hundred ȝer . atte chirche faste bi.
þe nome is seint Marie transpedi.
þer is þe piler þat peter and poul . was to bounde
668   And scourget . a swiþe gret stounde¹

At San Spirito,

² **A**t þe chirche . of seynt spirit.
In þe weie . to trismere ful riht.

daily, 800 years' pardon.

Vche dai þer is . eiȝte hundred ȝer to pardoun
672   And þridde part of þi sunnes . remissioun².

At St Mary Trastevere

³ At seinte Marie In trismere . þat ilke niht.
þat crist was boren . most of miht.
Sprong oyle . of a welle
676   As I. herde clerkes . in Rome telle

daily 2000 years' pardon.

Vche day . two þousend ȝer.
Of pardoun þou may haue þer ³.

*At St Gregory's 800 years.
At St Grisogono's 400 years.
At St Tyre and St John's 800 years' pardon, &c.*

At seint Gregories chirche þre hundred ȝer.⁴
680   And at seint grisogoni . four hundred is þer.⁷
In þᵉ chirche of seint tyre . and seint Ion.⁷
þer is Eiȝte hundred ȝer . to pardon.
And þridde part of þi sunnes . Remission.
684   To alle men . þat þider wol cum.
þat graunted þere . pope vrban.
To alle þat þere . þider cam.
þat weoren out of dedly synne.
688   þat pardon þere . may he wynne.

At St Lawrence's

At seint laurence in Damas.⁵

500 years.

fyf hundred ȝer . is in þat plas.

At St Bartholomew's 2000 years.

At seint bartelmeuȝ . þat holi Marter.⁶
692   þer is of pardoun . two þousend ȝer.

At St Angelo's

⁷ At seint Angel . as I. þe say

---

¹⁻¹ L. gives this, altered, at l. 810-17, p. 141-2.
²⁻² L. gives this, altered, at l. 818-21, p. 141. The Vernon MS. omits the L. St James, l. 822-5.
³⁻³ L. gives this, altered at l. 826-31, p. 142.
⁴ See L. l. 874-5, p. 143.   ⁵ L. l. 878-81, p. 143.
⁶ L. l. 742-5, p. 140.   ⁷⁻⁷ New. Not in L.

THE STACIONS OF ROME. (VERNON MS.) 23

	A þousend ȝer . þer haue þou may.	1000 years' pardon.
	Graunted of holi fadres . her bi-forn.	
696	To saue soules . þat weore for-lorn⁷.	
	¹At seint Marie rochel ȝif þou wolt craue	At St Mary Rochelle's 2000 years.
	two þousend ȝer . þer may þou haue ¹.	At St Peter's
	² At seint petres prisoun.	Prison 2000 years.
700	Two þousend ȝer . of pardoun².	[Fol. 315 b. col. 3.]
	And an hundred ȝer . at seint Adrian⁷.	At St Adrian's, and Sts Cosmo
	³ And as monye . at Cosma and Damian³.	and Damian's, 100 years each.
	A þousend ȝer . at seint Marie þe newe verrement,⁴	At St Mary the New 1000 years.
704.	And two þounsend ȝer . at seint Clement⁸.	At St Clement's 2000.
	A Mˡ· ȝer at seint Steuene certeynly ⁸.	At St Stephen's 1000.
	And at seint Andreuȝes . ȝeres þritti⁵.	At St Andrew's 30.
	⁶ At seint saluatour . to pardoun . Mˡ· ȝer.	At St Saviour's 1000 years.
708	Vche day in Bethleem . is granted þer.	
	Of Popus . þat þer han bene	
	To alle Men . þat ben clene	
	And to þat place . doþ eny good dede	
712	He schal hit haue . to his mede.	
	⁷At seint Alexto . ȝif þou wolt gon.	At St Alexto's (Alexis)
	þer þou maiȝt haue . to pardon.	
	Elleuene hundred ȝere	1100 years' pardon.
716	Vche day . þou maiȝt haue þere.	
	⁸ At a Chapel . of vre ladi.	At Our Lady's Chapel, where
	þer held scole seint Thomas of Canturburi.	Thomas à Becket kept school,
	viij .C. ȝer . is graunted þore.	800 years.
720	And at seint vrbans chirche . iiij þousend more.	At St Urban's, daily, 4384 years'
	Eueriche day . to pardoun.	pardon.
	And þridde part . þi sinnes remission.	
	And ȝit þer is . more ouere.	
724	þre hundred ȝere . foure score and and foure.	

¹⁻¹ L. l. 882-91, p. 144. ²⁻² L. l. 834-41, p. 142.
³ L. l. 848-9, p. 143. ⁴ L. l. 842-3, p. 142.
⁵ L. l. 896-906, p. 144. ⁶ L. l. 856-63, and see l. 3 above here.
⁷ L. l. 844-7, p. 142-3. ⁸⁻⁸ New. Not in L.

þat pardoun . popes þer han graunt.
To hem þat ben verrey repentaunt⁸.

So much pardon is there in Rome

728 ¹**I**N Rome . is muche pardoun more
þen I. haue told . here bifore

that I can't tell it.

Or telle schulde . wiþ al my miht.
þouh I. weore her . boþe day . and niht.

God grant us some of it,

Nou God . þat was . in Bedlem bore,
732 To saue þe world . þat was for-lore,
Graunt vs part . of þis pardoun.

and His blessing!

And þer to . his Benisoun . Amen.

¹ The end is slightly altered in L. l. 907-14, p. 144.

INDEX OF NAMES AND CHURCHES.

[The references preceded by **C.** refer to the Cotton Text, by **L.** to the Lambeth Text, as printed in *Political, Religious, and Love Poems*, E. E. T. Soc., 1866, 113—144. The other References are to this Vernon Text.]

Aaron, the rod of, p. 11, l. 321; **C.** p. 127, l. 392.
Adrian's, St, p. 23, l. 701.
Agrippa, p. 20, l. 619; **L.** p. 140, l. 754.
Alexto's, St, p. 23, l. 713; **L.** p. 142, l. 844.
Alisaundre, Pope, p. 2, l. 27; **C.** p. 114, l. 35; p. 6, l. 173; **C.** p. 121, l. 224.
Altars, the 7 chief at St Peter's, p. 2, l. 35; **C.** p. 115, l. 51.
Amas, St, **L.** p. 117, l. 111, note 1.
Ambrose's, St, **L.** p. 143, l. 875.
Ananias, p. 3, l. 79; **C.** p. 117, l. 111.
Anastace's, St, p. 4, l. 94; **C.** p. 117, l. 130; **L.** p. 131, top note.
Andrew, St, altar of, p. 2, l. 41.
Andrew's, St, p. 23, l. 706; **L.** p. 144, l. 896.
Angelo's, St, p. 22, l. 693.
Annes, St, **L.** p. 118, note 3.
Anthony's, St, p. 15, l. 473.
Anthonyne, Emperor, **L.** p. 135, l. 588; p. 15, l. 471; p. 18, l. 558.
Apostles, Church of, p. 19, l. 588; **L.** p. 139, l. 724.

Assumption-Day, **C.** p. 115, l. 75; p. 17, l. 529; **L.** p. 137, l. 649.
Austin's, St, p. 143, l. 875.
Bartholomew's, St, **L.** p. 140, l. 742; p. 22, l. 691.
Bastian's, St, p. 5, l. 147; **L.** p. 119, note 7; **C.** p. 120, l. 199.
Beatris's, St, p. 14, l. 413; **C.** p. 133, l. 536.
Benett, Pope, **L.** p. 119, note 7.
Bethlehem, p. 23, l. 708; p. 24, l. 731.
Blase, St, arm of, **L.** p. 139, l. 736.
Bonefas, Pope, p. 8, l. 231; p. 10, l. 285; **C.** p. 125, l. 348; p. 21, l. 637, 646; **L.** p. 141, l. 775, 789.
bones, 7000 holy, p. 14, l. 417.
brass, four Pillars of, from Jerusalem, **C.** p. 127, l. 408.
Cecilia's, St, p. 21, l. 663; **L.** p. 142, l. 832.
Cesar the martyr, **L.** p. 131, top note.
Chapels, 10,005 in Rome, **C.** p. 113, l. 20.

INDEX OF NAMES AND CHURCHES.

Childermas Day, p. 4, l. 87.
Christopher's arm, p. 15, l. 458; **L.** p. 135, l. 576.
Christ, mark of his footsole in Rome, p. 7, l. 211; **C.** p. 122, l. 252; relics of: his clothes, &c., p. 11, l. 329-338; p. 13, l. 381, &c.; p. 16, l. 491, &c.; **L.** p. 136, l. 607; **L.** p. 138, l. 698.
Clement's, St, p. 23, l. 704.
Clericorum, Chapel of, p. 12, l. 350.
Constance, p. 12, l. 369; **C.** p. 131, l. 482-5.
Constantyn, Kyng, p. 8, l. 243; **C.** p. 124, l. 304; p. 12, l. 370; p. 19, l. 591; **L.** p. 139, l. 726.
Cosmo's, St, p. 23, l. 702; **L.** p. 143, l. 848.
Cross, Christ's, p. 13, l. 386; **C.** p. 132, l. 499.
Cross, the penitent Thief's, p. 13, l. 388; **C.** p. 132, l. 501.

Damas, city of, p. 16, l. 481; **L.** p. 135, l. 597.
Damas, St Lawrence's in, p. 22, l. 689; **L.** p. 143, l. 878.
Damian's, St, p. 23, l. 702.
Demiave's (=Damian's), St, **L.** p. 143, l. 848.

Elene, St, p. 12, l. 372; **L.** p. 130, note §; **C.** p. 131, l. 481.
Eugenie, St, **L.** p. 139, l. 733.
Eusebius, St, p. 14, l. 439; **L** p. 134, l. 556.
Eustace's, St, p. 21, l. 655; **L.** p. 143, l. 850.

Fabian's, St, p. 5, l. 147; **C.** p. 120, l. 199.
Faustin's, St, p. 14, l. 413; **C.** p. 133, l. 536.
Friars Minors, **L.** p. 144, l. 890.

Gelasius, Pope, p. 6, l. 158; **C.** p. 120, l. 210.
Gregory, St, Altar of, p. 2, l. 42; gives pardon, p. 2, l. 48; p. 5, l. 150; p. 6, l. 172; p. 15, l. 463; p. 17, l. 526; **L.** p. 137, l. 646; p. 17, l. 539; **L.** p. 137, l. 663.
Gregory's, St, p. 22, l. 679; **L.** p. 143, l. 875.
Grisogoni's, St, p. 22, l. 680.
hay that Christ lay on before the ass, p. 16, l. 495; **L.** 136, l. 615.
Holy Roode chirche, p. 12, l. 367; **C.** p. 130, l. 478.
Honorius, Pope, p. 14, l. 431; **C.** p. 121, l. 225.

Innocent, Pope, p. 18, l. 559; **L.** p. 138, l. 693.

Jacob, St, p. 19, l. 599; **L.** p. 139, l. 732.
James's, St, p. 4, l. 92.
James's, St, uppon the Flome, **L.** p. 142, l. 822.
Jerome, St, p. 16, l. 479; **L.** p. 135, l. 596.
Jerusalem, p. 10, l. 291.
———, the Church, **C.** p. 130, l. 480, and Pref. **C.** p. xxxv.
John the Baptist, p. 8, l. 239; p. 9, l. 276; ashes of, p. 11, l. 330; **C.** p. 128, l. 417; chapel of, **C.** p. 125, l. 358.
John the Evangelist, p. 8, l. 238; p. 9, l. 275; **C.** p. 125, l. 338; chains of, **C.** p. 127, l. 408.
John Lateran, St, p. 8, l. 233; **C.** p. 123, l. 294.
John, Pope, p. 19, l. 593; **L.** p. 139, l. 728.
John the porte Latyn, St, **C.** p. 122, l. 268.
Julius, Emperor, p. 21, l. 640; **L.** p. 141, l. 780.

INDEX OF NAMES AND CHURCHES. 27

Julyan's, St, C. p. 134, l. 548; p. 15, l. 449; L. p. 135, l. 566.

Kateryne's, St, p. 10, l. 291; C. p. 125, l. 352.

kyrkes, 147 in Rome, C. p. 113, l. 18 (ii⁵ paresche churchs in the Porkington MS. No. 10).

Lammas, p. 3, l. 51; C. p. 115, l. 71; p. 19, l. 576; L. p. 139, l. 706.

Lawrence's, St, p. 13, l. 402; C. p. 132, l. 515.

Lawrence's, St, in Damace, p. 22, l. 689; L. p. 143, l. 778.

Lent, pardon doubled in, p. 3, l. 69.

Leo, Pope, altar of, p. 2, l. 43; bones of, C. p. 116, l. 96.

Loaves (?) and Fishes, relics of, p. 11, l. 326; C. p. 127, l. 397.

Luke, St, p. 17, l. 507; L. p. 136, l. 627.

Magdalene, Mary, her foot, C. p. 128, l. 425; p. 21, l. 664.

Mahoun, p. 8, l. 245; C. p. 124; l. 306.

Manna, p. 11, l. 325; C. p. 127, l. 396.

Marcelle's, St, p. 20, l. 610.

Martin, St, minster of, p. 3, l. 55; bed of, L. p. 130, l. 717.

Martin's, St, in the Mount, p. 18, l. 563.

Martyrs' Chapel, underground, p. 7, l. 181-200; C. p. 121, l. 233.

Mary, see Virgin.

Mary's, St, the Major, p. 16, l. 475; L. p. 135, l. 591.

Mary's, St, Merle, L. p. 144, l. 892.

Mary's, St, Nunciate, p. 5, l. 136; C. p. 119, l. 184.

Mary's, St, the New, p. 23, l. 703; L. p. 142, l. 842.

Mary's, St, Rochelle, p. 23, l. 697; L. p. 144, l. 882.

Mary's, St, the Round, p. 20, l. 613; L. p. 140, l. 746.

Mary's, St, Transpedi, p. 22, l. 666; L. p. 141, l. 810.

Mary's, St, Trismere, p. 22, l. 673; L. Tristmere or Tristiuere, p. 142, l. 826.

Mathewe's, St, p. 15, l. 454; L. p. 135, l. 573.

Maunde, p. 10, l. 306.

Modestus's, St, p. 15, l. 465; L. p. 135, l. 582.

nail of Christ's Cross, p. 13, l. 385; C. p. 131, l. 498.

Neptune, p. 20, l. 620, 629; L. p. 140, l. 755, 762.

Nichole, Pope, p. 6, l. 173; C. p. 121, l. 224.

Orban, Pope, L. p. 119, note 7.

Palmalle (print of Christ's footsole), p. 7, l. 201.

Palme, C. p. 122, l. 252.

Palmete, L. p. 122, note 2.

Pantheon, p. 20, l. 623; L. p. 140, l. 758.

pardon, explained, p. 1, l. 5-6.

Parnelle, St, C. p. 116, l. 97.

Paul, p. 1, l. 12; christened, p. 3, l. 80; stone he was beheaded on, p. 4, l. 109; p. 9, l. 276, 278; his head, p. 12, l. 357; his Prison, L. p. 142, l. 834.

Paul's, St, p. 3, l. 71; C. p. 116, l. 103.

Pelagius, Pope, p. 6, l. 171; p. 13, l. 405; C. p. 132, l. 518; p. 19, l. 593; L. p. 139, l. 728.

Peter, p. 1, l. 12; Peter's brother, p. 3, l. 81; p. 9, l. 276, 278; his head, p. 12, l. 357; his

Chapel, C. p. 114, l. 38; his Prison, p. 23, l. 699; L. p. 142, l. 834.
Peter, St, a Vincula, p. 19, l. 574; L. p. 138, l. 704.
Peter's, St, p. 2, l. 17; p. 6, l. 160; C. p. 114, l. 25; p. 20, l. 632; L. p. 140, l. 769.
Philip, St, p. 19, l. 599; L. p. 139, l. 372.
Pilate, Sire, p. 13, l. 391; C. p. 132, l. 504.
Pius, St, L. p. 138, l. 678.
Placidas, p. 21, l. 656.
Pope's Hall, the, p. 11, l. 342; C. p. 129, l. 441.
Popes, the Martyr-Popes' Chapel, p. 7, l. 181; C. p. 121, l. 233.
Praxed's, St, p. 18, l. 551.
Preselle's, St, L. p. 137, l. 662.
Presepe (boards from the Manger of the Nativity), p. 16, l. 484; L. p. 136, l. 600.
Purgatory, p. 14, l. 412.
Prudencian's, St p. 17, l. 536.
Pudencyam, L. p. 137, l. 656.

Relics, p. 10-11, p. 12-13; C. p. 126-8, p. 131-2; L. p. 139.
Rode (Christ's Cross), p. 12, l. 367; p. 13, l. 386; C. p. 130, l. 478; L. p. 139, l. 765.
Rome, p. 1, l. 4, 8, 10, &c., &c.
Romilous and Romilon, p. 1, l. 9.

Sabyne, St, p. 19, l. 601.
Sabasabyne, St, L. p. 139, l. 734.
Salvator (Crucifix), p. 12, l. 351; C. p. 126, l. 375; C. p. 130, l. 464; Chapel of, L. p. 143, l. 868.
Salvator, St, p. 18, l. 570; p. 21, l. 661.
Salvator's, St, p. 23, l. 707.
Sancta Sanctorum, p. 12, l. 349; C. p. 129, l. 462, and note 6, L.
San Spirito, church of, p. 22, l. 669.

Saul, p. 3, l. 75.
Scala Cœli, the Chapel, p. 5, l. 118; C. p. 118, 158.
Scherthorsday, p. 10, l. 307.
Sebastian, St, p. 6, l. 152.
Sebastian's, St, p. 5, l. 132; L. p. 120, note 3. *See* Bastian.
Sesyle's, St, L. p. 142, l. 832.
Silvester, Pope, p. 4, l. 103; p. 6, l. 172; p. 9, ll. 249, 277; p. 12, l. 375; C. p. 124, l. 310, 320.
Spirito, Santo, Hospital of, L. p. 142, l. 818.
Sponge offered to Christ, C. p. 131, l. 495.
Stephen, St, C. p. 116, l. 98; p. 133, l. 524.
Stephen's, St, p. 23, l. 705.
Stacions, The, p. 8, l. 230; C. p. 123, l. 291 : Preface, C. p. xxi.
Supper, the Last, Table of, p. 10, l. 325; C. p. 126, l. 380.
Symon, St, altar of, p. 2, l. 40.
Symple's, St, p. 14, l. 413; C. p. 133, l. 536-8.
Sysely's, St, L. p. 143, l. 864.

Tables of the Law, Moses's, p. 11, l. 317; C. p. 127, l. 388.
Thief, the penitent, his Cross, p. 13, l. 388.
Thomas's, St (the Apostle of India), p. 8, l. 217; C. p. 123, l. 278; p. 19, l. 602; L. p. 139, l. 735.
Thomas à Becket, relics of, p. 16, l. 497; L. p. 136, l. 618; his School, p. 23, l. 718.
Tiberian, the Emperour, p. 5, l. 126.
Titulus Pastoris, L. p. 138, l. 674.
Trismere, p. 22, l. 670, 673.
Tristiuere, or Tristmere, L. p. 142, l. 826.
Troy, Duchess of, p. 1, l. 7.

INDEX OF NAMES AND CHURCHES.

Urban, Pope, p. 4, l. 99; **L.** p. 134, note 1.
Urban's, St, p. 23, l. 720.

Vernicle, Altar of, p. 2, l. 37; pardon when V. showed, p. 3, l. 59; **C.** p. 116, l. 81; **C.** p. 128, l. 435.

Vevian's, St, p. 14, l. 427; **L.** p. 134, note 3.

Virgin Mary, second Chapel of, p. 5, l. 120-1; two chapels of, **C.** p. 118, l. 161; p. 5, l. 140;
day of her Assumption, **C.** p. 115, l. 75; her milk, **C.** p. 128, l. 424; her image, p. 16, l. 505; **L.** p. 136, l. 625; her chapel where Thomas à Becket kept school, p. 23, l. 717.

Vitus's, St, p. 15, l. 465; **L.** p. 135, l. 582.

Wells, the Three, from St Paul's blood, p. 4, l. 113; **C.** p. 118, l. 153.

St Kateryne, p. 10, l. 291; Polit., Rel., and Love Poems, p. 125, l. 352. The *Saturday Review* of Dec. 22, 1866, p. 765, col. 1, suggests that this is "no doubt St Katharine on Mount Sinai, mentioned along with Jerusalem as an alternative point within the Holy Land." The *Penny Cyclopædia* says, "In the midst of the [Sinai] hills, on the height of Jebel Musa, surrounded by higher mountain-tops, and near the summit considered as the proper Sinai of Scripture, is situated the convent of St Catherine, founded, according to the credited tradition, by Helena, the mother of Constantine, in the fourth century." The most approved Legend, says Mr Morton, makes her sister to Constantine (p. xi., Pref. to "The Legend of St Katherine of Alexandria," Abbotsford Club, 1841). The Virgin is said to have married this Saint to Jesus Christ; Maxentius (by some writers), or Maximinius (by others), is said to have tortured her, and put her to death. No contemporary writer mentions her (Morton, p. xi.).

Here bethe the stacyons of Rome.

[From Mrs Ormsby Gore's Porkington MS. No. 10, fol. 132, ab. 1460-70 A.D.]

IN rome bethe ij^C paresche churchs, & vij & x^C chapell*is* and v. The Cytty his about þ^e wallys xlij myllys, and oue*r* them byn ij ^{C} & lx tourr*is*. In þ^e Cetty byn xiiij prynssepall*e* gatt*is*. ¶ Be-fore þ^e mynst*ur* of sent pett*ur* ys A steyre of xxviij grecys. Pope Alysaundure granttyd vij ȝere of pardoñ at eue*ry* grece as hofte as anny mañ gothe hem w*i*tt [1] good dewocyon ; & aboufe þ^e grece-ys ys a chappell*e* alone, þ*a*t sente pett*ur* sannge in his furst mase. There ys vij M[1] ȝere of pardon, & so many lentt*is*, as oft as hit ys vesete w*i*tt devosyoñ. ¶ In þ^e mynst*ur* byn a C autorr*is*, & at eue*ry* aut*ur* ys xxviij ȝere of pardon, and so mony lentt*is* grau*n*t at þ^e havllowynge by þ^e sayde pope. [2] But vij byn moche & most of dygnyte, þ*a*t is to say, furst on þ^e ryȝtt hond ys þ^e aut*ur* of þ^e varnacull*e*. ¶ The ij of þ^e honoure of oure lady : The þred of sent symon & Iude : The iiij of cent androw : The v of sent gregorye, and þe*r* he lythe : The vj of sent leoo þ^e pope : The vij of þ^e holly cros, & þe*r*in commythe no woman. And Euery aut*ur* ys eue*ry* day vij ^{C} ȝer*e*, & so mony lentt*is*, of pardoñ. ¶ And at þ^e hy haut*ur* ys fore-ȝeyfnys of synnys þ*a*t be fore-

St Peter's.
There are 100 steps,

[1 MS. wtt *all through*]

and 100 altars,

[2 Fol. 132 *b*.] whereof 7 are Chief Altars,

at each of which is great pardon, but more at the High Altar.

THE STACYONS OF ROME. (PORKINGTON MS.) 31

gettyn, & fowys¹, & xxviij ȝere of pardon granttyde of [¹ ? MS. ? =faults]
gregory þᵉ pope: from holly-roode daye to lammas ys
euery day xiiij M¹ ȝere of pardon. ¶ Oñ our lady On the Assumption of Our Lady,
day þᵉ somsyon ys a M¹ [ȝ]ere of pardoñ ¶ On sent 1000 years' pardon.
pettur and paullis day ys ij M¹ ȝer of pardoñ ¶ On
sent marttayn þᵉ vij day was þat place hallowyd. Then
ys xxviij M¹ ȝere of pardoñ, & so mony lenttis, &
þᵉ þrede part & of pennance vndo ¶ When they Of the Pardon when the Verschowe þᵉ warnakoll, ys iiij M¹ ȝere of pardon; to nicle is shown.
pepule of oþer placys ix M¹; & ȝefe he pase þᵉ see
xiiij M¹, & þᵉ þrede part of synnys fore-²geyve ¶ [² Fol. 133.]
And in Lent euery pardoñ ys dovbullyd³ ¶ And þer [³ ll crossed, as for e]
byñ holly bonnys of seynt pettur, & poulle,³ & symond, Bones of Sts Peter, Paul,
& iude, gregorye, lyoñ, pernell, & oþer mo : þᵉ pardoñ Pernelle, &c.
can no mañ tell þat þer is ¶ Frow sent pettur vn-to
poulles is iij myle : to þat pardouñ þe pardoun fulle St Paul's.
gret ¶ And in þᵉ conuercyoun of paulle is ij M¹
ȝere, & in his daye I M¹ ȝere, & at chyldormas day in
crystynmas ij M¹ ȝere. On sent mertayn þᵉ Xiij day
þat mynsteyre was hallowyd : Then ys xxviij M¹
ȝere of pardoun, & þᵉ þrede part of pennance vndo ; & he
þat is þer euery sondaye in þᵉ ȝere haþe as moche pardon as ȝeyf he went to señt Iamis ¶ Frow sent [³ ll crossed, as for e]
paullis³ to sente austens is ij myle of feyre waye : þer is St Austin's.
euery day viij M¹ ȝere of pardoun, & þᵉ þred part of
paynance vndo, granttyd by pope vrban ; & sylvester
grant for-geyfnis of wrathe-þinge of fadore & modore, so
he layde no vyolent honde on hem ¶ Be-fore þᵉ dore The Stone that St Paul's head
ys þᵉ ston þat sent paullis hede lay on ; & þer be iij lay on.
wellis³ of gret vertu ¶ And þer ys ⁴A chappelle þat [⁴ Fol. 133 b.]
men calle schalla cely, þat ys of oure lady, & fele holly Schalla Cely.
bonnys byñ vndur þᵉ autur, x M¹ merturis in þᵉ tyme
of tybure-rya þᵉ emparoure. he þat saythe a mase þer A mass said there brings a soul
witt good devossyoñ may brynge a soule out of pul- from Purgatory.
catorry to heyvyñ, & gretly helpe his frende þat is
alyue . & iij M¹ ȝere of pardon ys granttyde by popys

[¹ MS. *faded*]	xlvij þat liue at sent sebestyande¹. Co*n*formyde be vrbane, seluest*er*, be*n*net, leoñ,· & clement ¶ Frowe
Our Lady the Annunciate.	sent austens to oure lady þᵉ anu*n*cyat ys ij loñge myle : þ*er* ys v C ȝere of pardoñ. A meraculle of oure lady was þ*er* schewyde ¶ Fro sent marye anu*n*cyant to
St Fabian's and Bastian's.	fabyan & bestyan þ*er* aperyd a nangelle to señt gregory at þᵉ hyȝhe autu*r*· at mase, & sayde þ*er* was reymyssioñ granttyde of gode, xl M¹ ȝere of pardoñ ; & so mony lentt*is* pope pallagyus ȝaffe þerto ¶ There lay pett*ur* & paule ij C ȝere ore they were fonde : þ*er* is more pardo*n* þen is at señt pett*ur*is ȝefe of dyue*r*is pop*is*,
[² Fol. 134.] *The Martyr-Popes' Chapel*	for þat place is havllowyd w*itt* þᵉ bo*n*n*is* ²of mo*n*ny seyntt*is*. A lyttylle be syde ys a chappelle, & þ*er* lyne xxviij pop*is* ma*r*tu*r*is, & þ*er* is playñ reymyssioñ, & he þat dyithe þᵉde*r*-warde schall be sawyde fore his good
under-ground.	entent. ¶ Thus chappell ys vnde*r* þᵉ grou*n*d, & me*n* most go to hit w*itt* ca*n*dyl lyȝte ; fore su*m* tyme me*n* þat we*r* holly, hyde þem þer*i*n to do gret pe*n*nau*n*ce
St John Lateran.	fore þᵉ love of gode ¶ Frowe fabyañ & bestyañ to sent Iohñ þᵉ lattron: þ*er* is pardoñ granttyd be þᵉ prayere of sent Iohñ þᵉ va*n*gelyst, þ*er* is not more pardoñ in alle rome, & be þᵉ preyere of sent Iohñ þᵉ Babtyste
The Emperor Constantine converted by Silvester.	¶ The Emparoure Costantyñ was co*n*uertyd by pope sylvest*ur* ; he ȝaufe hym his palles to make hit þᵉ hous of gode, & þᵉ holly pope syluest*ur* ȝaufe þerto pardon to he*m* þat is cleyne confessyde, & reypentau*n*ce of his sy*n*ne, & vesettythe þat place devotly ; as cleyn as þᵉ soule parttythe frow þᵉ flesche, so cleyn he be of alle his sy*n*nys ; & as sent bonyface wytnyssythe, he þat
[³ Fol. 134 *b*.] *Christ's Table, and Moses's Tables of stone.*	wyll truly fette pardou*n*, ³they nedythe not to go to þᵉ holly land. ¶ There is þᵉ tabulle þat cryst made on his mau*n*day, & ij tabulle*is* þat he made w*itt* his one hond, & wrōt his law*is* þat he toke to moysses ; & þᵉ clothis of señ Iohñ, & þᵉ scherte þat cryst weriyde, þat oure lady mad ; & þᵉ syrcu*m*syse of crystys flesche.
St Saviour's. [⁴ MS. *senatoure*.]	¶ There ys a chappell of sent seuatoure⁴ : eue*r*y day

THE STACYONS OF ROME. (PORKINGTON MS.)

ix Mͥ ȝere of pardoñ ys at þat place ¶ There ys a
saluatur þat was sent to oure lady froo heyvyñ. And
sent syluestur clossyd þᵉ¹ heddis of pettur & poull in   [¹ MS. þe þe]
þᵉ hy autur on sent Iohñnys day yᵉ ȝere of oure lorde a
Mͥ CCC & iij ȝere, & hit fell oñ a þorsday, & in þᵉ rofe
ouer þᵉ popys see ys a fayre saluatur þat neuer vas
peynt witt mans honde ¶ And at þᵉ chappell of þᵉ holly   *Holy Rood Chapel.*
rood ys euery sonday & wennisday ij C & 1 ȝere, &
euery daye a C ȝere to pardoñ ¶ At sent lavrence ys   *St Lawrence's.*
euery day vij Mͥ ȝere of pardoñ, & so mony lenttis, &
fore-ȝeyfnys of pennance vndo : & who-so be euery
Wennnysday þer in þᵉ ȝere, he hathe þᵉ grace of gode to
²be in cleyn lyue. þat place hallowyd sent gregorye   [² Fol. 135.]
¶ At sent Benyan þat lythe [neer] sent gellyañ, þer is   *St Benyan's. (Vivian's ?)*
a C ȝere of pardoñ ¶ At sent vytte & modesce ys for-   *St Vitus and Modestus's.*
geyfnys of þᵉ iiij part of youre synnys ¶ At sent   *St Antony's.*
antony ys fore-ȝefnys of þᵉ viij parte of synnys. ¶ At
sent praxsede þᵉ iiij parte of synnys ys fore-geyf ¶   *St Praxed's.*
At sent mary þᵉ maioure, at þᵉ hy autur ys þᵉ body of   *St Mary the Greater.*
sent maþewe & Ierone þᵉ holly doctur, & a nare of sent
Thomas þᵉ merttur, & his breyñ, & a rocket þat was   Thomas à Becket's relics.
spronge witt his blod þat he werryd at his takynge, &
of þᵉ hey þat cryst lay in be-fore þᵉ asse : & þer is a
ymage of oure lady, of angellis werke ¶ At sent
prudencian byn hyriud v Mͥ marturis. þer is fore-
geyfnys of þᵉ iij parte of synne, & fore euery body of
þem is a C ȝere & xl dayis pardoñ ¶ At þᵉ mount of   *St Martin's Mount.*
sent marttayñ ys vij ᶜ ȝere to pardoñ ¶ At sent
pettur þᵉ ad vyncula euery day iij ᶜ ȝere to pardoñ, & at   *St Peter ad Vincula.*
lammas fulle reymyssyoñ ¶ At alle þᵉ paleis, at euery
apos³ tyllys day ys iij Mͥ ȝere of pardon ¶ At sent   [³ Fol. 136, back]
mary þᵉ rounde ys a churche vndure þᵉ vrthe ; & þer   *St Mary the Round.*
þᵉ xiiij day of may & alle haullowyn day, is fulle rey-
missyoñ, & euery day I Mͥ ȝere of pardon. ¶ At
sent austens lythe placydas þat was callyd, & nowe he   *St Austin's.*
ys sent Eusstas, & his wyfe, & his iij sonnys vndure

þᵉ hy autur; pope pylagius grauntide iij Mˡ ʒere of
[ˡ sent dotted out] pardoñ ¶ At ˡþᵉ blacke saluatur be iij Mˡ ij C
The Black Salvator.
St Cecilia's.
St Mary's in Trasponti.
& xl ʒere of pardoñ. ¶ At sent Celce ys I C ʒere of pardon : þer is a foott of mary mavdelen ¶ At sent mary in trasponti is ij C ʒere of pardoñ, Et C.

Explycyt tractus de indulgencia romana siue apostolica. ·:

The Pilgrims Sea-Voyage.

(From the Trin. Coll., Cambridge, MS. R, 3, 19, t. Hen. VI.)

A SUPPLEMENT TO
"THE STACIONS OF ROME."

The Pilgrims Sea-Voyage and Sea-Sickness.

From Trinity College Library MS. R, 3, 19, temp. Hen. VI.

    Men may leue alle gamys,   *You leave all fun behind you when you sail to St James's!*
    That saylen to seynt Jamys!
    Ffor many a man hit gramys¹,
4   When they begyn to sayle.
    Ffor when they haue take the see,   *Directly you get on board*
    At Sandwyche, or at Wynchylsee.
    At Brystow, or where that hit bee.
8   Theyr hertes begyn to fayle.   *your heart fails,*

    Anone the mastyr commaundeth fast   *the shipmen make ready,*
    To hys shyp-men in alle the hast,
    To dresse hem sone about the mast,
12   Theyr takelyng to make.
    With "howe! hissa!" then they cry,   *hollow,*
    "What, howe, mate! thow stondyst to ny,   *order you out of their way.*
    Thy felow may nat hale the by;"
16   Thus they begyn to crake².

    A boy or tweyñ Anone up styen,
    And ouerthwart the sayle-yerde lyen;—
    "Y how! taylia!" the remenaunt cryen,   *and haul at the sails.*
20   And pulle with alle theyr myght.

¹ A.S. *gram*, troublesome; *gramian*, to anger.
² to boast, hector.

"Put the boat ready; our Pilgrims will groan ere night."	"Bestowe[1] the boote, Bote-swayne, anoñ, That our pylgryms may pley theron ; For som ar lyke to cowgh and grone 24 Or hit be full mydnyght.
"Haul up the bowline! Poor Pilgrims, can't eat! Steward, a pot of beer!	"Hale the bowelyne[2]! now, vere the shete[3]!— Cooke, make redy anoon our mete, Our pylgryms haue no lust to ete, 28 I pray god yeue hem rest!" "Go to the helm! what, howe! no nere[4]? Steward, felow! A pot of bere!" "Ye shalle have, sir, with good chere, 32 Anoñ alle of the best."

"Y howe! trussa! hale in the brayles[5]!
Thow halyst nat, be god, thow fayles!

[1] I suppose that *Bestowe* has not here its present provincial meaning of *Stow away*.

[2] *Bowling*, or rather *Bow-line*, is a Rope made fast to the Leetch, or middle part of the out-side of a Sail, by two, three, or four other Ropes like a Crow's Foot, which is termed the *Bowling-bridle;* the use of it being to make the Sails stand sharp, or close, or by a Wind. *Sharp the main Bowlings, Hale up* or *set taught the Bowling,* are Sea-phrases us'd when the Bowling is to be pull'd up harder, or hal'd forwards on : And To *ease, cheek,* or *run up the Bowling,* is to let it out more slack. Phillips.

[3] To *Veer out a Rope,* is to put it out by Hand, or to let it run out of itself ; as *Veer more Cable, i.e.* let more of it run out · But this Word is not apply'd to any Running-Rope except the Sheats. *Sheats* (in a Ship) are Ropes bent to the Clews of the Sails, which serve in all the lower Sails to *hale aft* or *round off* the Clew of the Sail ; but in the Top-Sails they are made use of to *hale home, i.e.* to draw close the Sail to the Yard-Arms (Those Planks under Water, which come along the *Run* of the Ship, and are clos'd to the Stern-post, are also call'd *Sheats*). To *Ease the Sheat,* is to *veer* it out, or to let it go out gently. To *Let fly the Sheat* is to let it run out violently, as far as it will go : so that the Sail will then hang loose, and hold no Wind. Phillips.

[4] no nearer, that is, don't go closer to the wind. G. M. Hantler.

[5] *Brails* (Sea-term), small Ropes put thro' Blocks, or Pulleys fasten'd on either side of the Ties, so that they come down before the Sails of a Ship ; their use being, when the Sail is furled across,

THE PILGRIMS SEA-VOYAGE AND SEA-SICKNESS. 89

     O se howe welle owre good shyp sayles!"   *How well she sails!*
36   And thus they say among.
"Hale in the wartake ¹!" "hit shal be done."   *Steward, lay the cloth;*
"Steward! couer the boorde anone,
And set bred and salt therone,   *give 'em bread and salt for*
40   And tary nat to long."   *dinner."*

Then cometh oone and seyth, "be mery;   *"Storm's coming."*
Ye shall haue a storme or a pery."
"Holde thow thy pese! thow canst no whery,
44   Thow medlyst wondyr sore."
Thys mene whyle the pylgryms ly,   *The poor Pilgrims have their bowls*
And haue theyr bowlys fast theym by,   *by them, and cry out for hot*
And cry aftyr hote maluesy,   *Malmsey;*
48   "Thow helpe for to restore."

And som wold haue A saltyd tost,
Ffor they myght ete neyther sode ne rost;   *they can neither eat boiled nor*
A man myght sone pay for theyr cost,   *roast.*
52   As for oo day or twayne.
Som layde theyr bookys on theyr kne,
And rad so long they myght nat se;—
"Allas! myne hede wolle cleue on thre!"   *"My head will split in three,"*
56   Thus seyth another certayne.   *says one.*

to hale up its Bunt that it may be the more readily taken up or let fall. *Hale up the Brails*, or *Brail up the Sails*, an expression us'd by Sea-men when they would have the Sails hal'd up in order to be furled, or bound close to the Yard. Phillips.

¹ There is no such word in our modern sea-terms. If *war* is the *war* of *war*fare, *take* may mean tackle, and refer to some nettings or apparatus outside the vessel. But if, as is more probable, the *take* means *tack*, the rope running from the clew or corner of the lower square-sail, to fasten it inboard through a ring or the like in the deck—(the sheet runs also from the corner, but fastens the sail outside the bulwark, through which it runs to a cleat inside)—then *war* may mean left or right [? *guard*], according to the tack to be hauled in. The *bowline* runs from the perpendicular edge of the sail, a third down, to the mast in front, and pulls the sail against the wind so as to keep it bellied. G. M. Hantler.

The shipowner comes		Then cometh owre owner lyke a lorde.
		And speketh many A Royall worde,
to see that all's right.		And dresseth hym to the hygh borde,
	60	To see alle thyng be welle.
		Anone he calleth a carpentere,
		And byddyth hym bryng with hym hys gere,
The cabins are made ready.		To make the cabans here and there,
	64	With many a febylle celle ;
No sack of straw even for you!		A suk of strawe were there ryght good,
		Ffor som must lyg theym in theyr hood ;
		I had as lefe be in the wood,
	68	Without mete or drynk ;
		For when that we shall go to bedde,
And the pump, my goodness, stinks enough to kill you!		The pumpe was nygh oure beddes hede,
		A man were as good to be dede
	72	As smell therof the stynk !

EXPLICIT.

Clene Maydenhod.

(From the Vernon MS., ab. 1370 A.D., in the Bodleian Library, Oxford.)

A SUPPLEMENT TO
"HALI MEIDENHAD,"
(Early English Text Society, 1866.)

EDITED BY
FREDERICK J. FURNIVALL, M.A.,
TRIN. HALL, CAMBRIDGE.

LONDON:
PUBLISHED FOR THE EARLY ENGLISH TEXT SOCIETY,
BY N. TRÜBNER & CO., 60, PATERNOSTER ROW.

MDCCCLXVII.

Of Clene Maydenhod.

[Vernon MS. (ab. 1370 A.D.) fol. 299, col. 3 ; seventeen stanzas of eights. The stops are the metrical points and single-letter guards of the MS. The hyphens are the Editor's.]

Of clene Maydenhod.
To be weddet clanly to god.

Oᴠ A trewe loue . clene *and* derne.
Ichaue I.-write þe A Ron.   *I tell you how to love your Love.*
How þou maiȝt . ȝif þow wolt lerne.
4 For to loue . þi lemmon.
þat trewest is . of alle berne.
And most of loue . chacche con.
Beo war . for he is sumdel steorne.
8 His eȝe is euere . þe vppon.
þou art wrouht . of such a kynde.
Wiþ-outen loue . maiȝt þou not be.
And neuer more . schalt þou fynde.   *None is so sweet and fair as He.*
12 þat is so swete . and feir as he.
Ȝif þou miht hym . to þe bynde.
Wiþ trewe loue . bondes þre.
Wiþ al þin herte . wille . *and* mynde
16 From þe . wol he neuer fle
¶ Heddest þou founden . such a feere.   *He is fairer than Absalom, stronger than Samson.*
þat weore so feir . as Absolon.
And þer-to . so strong to tere   [Fol. 299 b. col. 1.]
20 As in his tyme . was Sampson.

l. 1, derne; A.S. *dearn,* secret.
l. 2, Ron ; A.S. *run,* a letter, talk.   l. 6, chacche, ? catch, take.
l. 17, feere, mate, companion.   l. 19, þer-to, also.

OF CLENE MAYDENHOD.

richer and wiser than Solomon.	So Riche þer-to . þat he were.
	And so wys . as Salomon.
	I.-wis to him . riht nouȝt hit were.
	24 þat þou hast chosen . to þi lemmon.
Man's love is	¶ For monnes loue . ȝif þou beo holde.
	Hit lasteþ . but a luytel res.
	And wiþ gyle . is al bi-folde.
fickle and false.	28 Hit is Fikel . Fals and les.
	Whon þou wenest . hit best to holde.
	Hit wendeþ a-wey . as wyndes bles.
	And bi-comeþ . wrest and colde.
	32 For trewe loue . hit neuer nes.
Man's love	¶ Loue þat wol not . wiþ þe a-byde.
	And þou hit desyre . þou hast wouh.
	Ar þou beo war . hit wol to-glyde.
	36 Hit is fikel . Fals . and Frouȝ.
is never constant;	Hit is a-weyward . In vche¹ a syde
	Whiles hit lasteþ . vnwrest and wouh.
	Beo war . and seo . what wol be-tyde
blows off as leaf on bough. Put then away man's love,	40 Hit wol to-dryue . as lef on bouh.
	¶ þe loue þat wole . to serwe wende.
	þou do hit al . out of þi pouȝt.
bind Christ in thy heart.	And his loue . in þin herte bynde
	44 þat haþ þi loue . so deore a-bouȝt.
	For ȝif þou heddest . al to þe ende.
	Heuene and eorþe . þorwȝ-out souht.
	To fynde a feere . þat weore so hende.
	48 As he . I.-wys hit weore for nouȝt.
He is meek,	¶ He is of Mood . wel Meke and Mylde.
	Freo of herte . strong of miht.
	Of glade chere . of wordes vn-wylde.
lovely of face,	52 Of louesum leore . and Eiȝen briht.

¹ MS. adds in vch.

l. 26, res; A.S. ræs, course, race.   l. 28, les; A.S. leas, counterfeit, loose.   l. 31, wrest; ? A.S. wræst, delicate, gentle.
l. 36, Frouȝ, frough, loose, spongy, brittle. (Halliwell.)

OF CLENE MAYDENHOD.

    Ȝif þou wolt do þe . in his mylde
    And him al-one . loue ariht.
    With-Inne þin herte . wol he bylde
56 And wone wiþ þe . boþe day and niht.   *ever constant.*
¶ Wel more murþe . is in his steuen.
    Þen herte may þenke . or tonge neme.
    As be þe swan . þe blake Rauen.
60 Also be him . þe sonne gleme.   *He is brighter than the sun;*
    No more is no þing . to him I.-lyche.
    Þen Galle is . to þe hony streme.
    Of him is al þe Ioye . of heuene-riche   *He is the joy of heaven.*
64 Þat with his grace . alle þing wol leme.
¶ Ȝif Mon be ded . and he him Ryne.   *He raises the dead to life.*
    He reiseþ him . to lyue anone
    For wele *and* wynne . serwe and pyne.
68 Al is Buxom . to him one
    Ȝif þow him wole . in herte wel tyne.
    And kepe þat he . not from þe gon
    Holde him . wiþ loue lyne.   *Love's bonds alone hold Him.*
72 For oþer bond . holdeþ him non.
¶ Is non founden . here in londe.   *None is so rich as He;*
    Þat is so Riche Mon . of Fee
    For more good . he haþ in honde.
76 Þen herte may þenke . or eiȝe mai se.
    Nis kyng . kniht . sweyn . ne bonde.   *He is over all.*
    Þat heo to him . mote Boxum be
    He haþ I.-send . a derne sonde   *He desires thy love;*
80 And desyreþ to haue þe loue of þe.
¶ He askeþ wiþ þe . nouþer lond ne leode.   *He asks no dower with thee ;*
    Gold ne seluer . ne precious stone.
    To such þinges . haþ he no neode
84 Al þat is good . is wiþ hym one

l. 53, mylde ; A.S. *milde*, mercy, pity.
l. 58, neme ; A.S. *nemnan*, name.   l. 64, leme ; A.S. *leoman*, enlighten.   l. 65, Ryne ; A.S. *rynan*, whisper.
l. 67, wynne ; A.S. *wyn*, pleasure.   l. 68, buxom ; A.S. *buhsom*, obedient.   l. 69, tyne ; A.S. *tynan*, to hedge in, enclose.

OF CLENE MAYDENHOD.

He gives thee Heaven,

paved with gold,

where no night is,

if thou wilt love Him, Christ. For this,

[Fol. 299 b. col. 2.]
keep thyself chaste,

pure under petticoat.

Nothing does God love more than Maidenhood,

which once lost, can never be found again.

All the gold of Arabye

  3if þou wiþ him . þi lyf wolt lede
  And graunte to ben . his owne lemmon.
  I . wot ful wel . what worþ þi meede.
88 Forsoþe . þe heuene riche won.
 ¶ þe weyes ben alle . þere I.-bete.
  Wiþ Riche gold . þat schyneþ briht.
  þe Ioyful song . in vche a strete
92 þer is day . and neuer more niht.
  To synge . wol þei neuer lete.
  To worschupe god . wiþ al heore miht.
  þat Blisse forsoþe . schal be þe mete.
96 3if þou Ihesu crist . loue ariht.
 ¶ 3if þou wolt . þi lemmon qweme.
  And to his brihte boure be brou3t.
  In Chastite . kep þou þe clene.
100 þat þou ne be . I.-wemmed nouht.
  Non hony Com . þat renneþ on streme
  Was neuer 3ut . so swete wrouht.
  Ne neuere so briht . sonne gleme.
104 þen Mayden . þat is clene of þou3t.
 ¶ While þou art clene . vnder gore.
  Bi-fore God . þou art ful hei3e
  þer is no þing . he loueþ more
108 þen Maidenhod . to wonen him nei3e
  Ne lerne þou neuere . þat ilke lore
  Wher þorw þou leose . Mayden Bei3e.
  þe þing þat mon . may fynde no more.[1]
112 Bot he hit kepe . he is vn-sle3e.
 ¶ þau3 al þe gold . of Arabye.
  Riche Rynges . and 3ymmes stone.

[1] See the Burlesque Recipe to restore Maidenhood in *Reliquiæ Antiquæ*, vol. i. p. 250-1, A.D. 1520

l. 87, worþ, shall be. l. 93, lete; A.S. *lætan*, leave.
l. 97, qweme ; A.S. *cweman*, please. l. 100, Iwemmed; A.S. *wem*, a spot; *wemme*, stained. l. 110, Bei3e; A.S. *beåh*, ring, crown.
l. 112, vnsle3e, unsly, foolish. l. 114, 3ymmes stone, gem stones. See l. 121.

OF CLENE MAYDENHOD.

       And all þe tresour . of Asye.   *and Asye*
116 Of oþer londes . euerichone.
       Weore bi-taken . in þi Baylye
       To welden and hauen . in þi wone
       Hit neore nouȝt . to þe druwerie   *are nothing worth by the side of*
120 Of clene Maidenhod . al one.   *Maidenhood.*
    ¶ Hose . þis ȝeem ston miht.   *Whoever preserves this*
       Louken . in a swete loue ryng.
       He schulde schyne . also briht.
124 As sonne doþ . wiþ-outen endyng.
       And beo holden . a ful swete wiht.
       Bi-fore god . [and] al Monkynde.
       þat wolde . in a Mayden liht.   *is held full sweet by Christ.*
128 Ful swete hit is . of hire þe Muynde.
    ¶ Lord ȝif us . miht and grace.   *Lord, give us grace to live*
       Chaste lyf . þat we ne spille.   *chaste lives,*
       Verrey compungcion . and space.
132 Repentaunce . of dedes ille
       And ȝif vs miht . to folwe þi trace.   *and follow Thy footsteps!*
       Euer more . boþe loude and stille.
       þat to þe siht . of þi swete face.
136 On domes day . we may come tille.

l. 119, druwerie; O. Fr. *druerie, drurie*, amitié, attachement, amour, passion; de l' ahal (Old High German), *trût, drût*, aujourd' hui *traut*, dilectus. Burguy.
    l. 121, hose, whoso.   l. 128, Muynde; A.S. *myne*, thought, memory.

The manufacturer's authorised representative in the EU for product safety is Oxford University Press España S.A. of El Parque Empresarial San Fernando de Henares, Avenida de Castilla, 2 - 28830 Madrid (www.oup.es/en or product.safety@oup.com). OUP España S.A. also acts as importer into Spain of products made by the manufacturer.
Printed and bound by CPI Group (UK) Ltd, Croydon, CR0 4YY
20/03/2026
02075339-0002